BANG BANG BEIRUT

(OR "STAND BY YOUR BEDOUIN")

A FARCE IN THREE ACTS BY

RAY COONEY and TONY HILTON

ENGLISH THEATRE GUILD LTD

1 THE PAVEMENT

LONDON SW4 0HY

For information regarding the acting fee payable on each and every amateur performance of this play throughout the world, and any other particulars, application must be made to the publishers:—

ENGLISH THEATRE GUILD LTD.

LONDON

No performance can be given unless a licence is first of all obtained.

Fees are payable in advance.

Licences will be issued on receipt of remittance provided the following details are forwarded :

    Date or dates of performance.
    Name of theatre or hall and full address.
    Name of Society.

Application for permission to give professional repertory performances of this play must be made to English Theatre Guild Ltd., at the above address.

© Copyright : Ray Cooney and Tony Hilton, 1971.

Costumes can be obtained from Charles H. Fox Ltd., 25 Shelton Street, London, W.C.2.

Act 1

ON STAGE	OFF STAGE

ON STAGE

Telephone on reception counter.

Theatrical basket

OFF STAGE

Silencer gun from pocket—Spence.

Long, curved knife—Arab.

Wallet, passport, watch and ring from Spence's body.

Umbrella—Fred.

Handbag containing driving licence, plane tickets and £250 in notes—Tracy.

Hip flask—Stanley.

Wazir's Luggage, golfclubs, tennis racquets, etc.—Hamid.

Drinks trolley with drinks, glasses, soda syphon—Hamid.

Military cane—Abu.

Act 2

ON STAGE

Pencil for Wooley.
Drinks and glasses, etc.
Fred's theatrical basket/trunk containing wig, cap and Long John Silver hat.

OFF STAGE

Golf club—Wazir.

'Suspencer-belt armoury'—Tracy.

Pills—Tracy.

Earring—Tracy.

Fountain pen, cigar, lighter, copy of "Snow White", toilet bag, talcum powder, deodorant, toothbrush, pipel cigarettes, self-inflating dinghy, suicide pill contained in suitcase—Tracy.

Two trays of food (one with a wineglass)—Hamid.

Tennis racquet—Wazir.

Scrap of yellow rubber—Fred.

Gun—Tracy.

Table napkin—Wazir.

Syringe from skirt—Tracy.

Duster—Hamid.

Gun—Eloise.

Act 3

Squash racquet—Wazir.

Suitcase (containing same things as in Act 2—Fred.

Knife—King.

Glass of Brandy—Stan.

Lighter—Stan.

Brooch—Eloise.

Bracelet with removable stone—Tracy.

Syringe—Tracy.

Aerosol spray—Tracy.

Woollen dressing gown and schoolboy cap for Fred.

Handkerchief—Fred.

Hip-flask—Stan.

Pistol—Abu.

Sten gun—Soldier.

Wazir's squash racquet—Fred.

AUTHORS' NOTES

The revolving radio room-cum-reception desk need not be as complicated as indicated in the script. It can simply be a sliding panel which reveals the radio room or, alternatively, just a sliding panel with no transmitting equipment seen at all. The panel would slide left or right and the actors would exit turning either one way or the other. If either of these methods are used by drama groups it will obviously be necessary to slightly alter the stage directions and speeches accordingly.

In Act II the dinghy is inflated by connecting the valve to an air-pipe which is hidden in the back of the stone seat. The pipe leads off to an air cylinder off-stage R. The actor playing FRED surreptitiously connects and then disconnects the valve. As there are plenty of good laughs in the sequence its not too difficult to choose the moment!

BANG BANG BEIRUT

ACT ONE

SETTING

The Lounge and Courtyard of a small and dingy hotel some-where in the Middle East. The Courtyard section leads from down right to almost up right centre. Running along the back of the Courtyard is a low ornamental wall, beyond which is the desert. Down right of the Courtyard is a small archway leading off to the main hotel entrance. In the centre of the Courtyard is a stone seat. There is a flight of stairs which runs up centre in the Courtyard along the back wall of the Lounge. Immediately facing the top of the stairs is a curtained archway leading off to the bedrooms. To the right of the stairs is an arched opening overlooking the Courtyard and at the far end of the landing is a bedroom door. U.L. is a large grandfather clock. Under the landing is the reception counter on which is an old fashioned telephone and behind this counter a small exchange board together with the usual clutter of items used at a reception desk. Later in the action of the play this whole reception counter and the wall behind swings round to reveal a radio-communication room. There are two arches in the left, wall. The Upstage arch leads to Kitchen and cellars. The Downstage arch leads to Dining Room and Bar. Persian carpets decorate the floors and walls. In the back wall U.L.C. can be seen the shuttered windows of the Bedroom about 10 feet from the ground. The Shutters can open and the interior of the Bedroom can be seen. Down L. is set a theatrical basket with "Fred Florence" on it.

TIME: Nine o'clock in the evening.

The Courtyard is lit by moonlight and the last rays of the setting sun. The Lounge is in eerie shadows and, at the moment, empty. In the distance can be heard the 'wailing' of the 'Faithful' engaged in Evening Prayer. After a moment a man climbs the low wall and drops into the Courtyard; it is JOHN SPENCE. He is followed by a young ARAB BOY whom he helps over the wall. He motions to the boy to be quiet and looks back over the wall to the right and left. Crosses the Courtyard into the Lounge and up the staircase and along to the bedroom door at the left hand end of the landing. Here SPENCE gives a 'Special Knock' and after a moment the door opens and TRACY appears, lit by the light from the bedroom behind her.

SPENCE indicates in dumb show for her to take the ARAB BOY into the bedroom while he stays out on the landing. TRACY mimes 'why?', SPENCE points towards the Courtyard and ushers her into the bedroom. He comes quickly down into the Lounge and goes stealthily out into the Courtyard. He takes a 'Silencer' from his pocket and affixes it to his gun. He then moves quietly over to the Reception Desk and crouches down beside it. After a moment the face of an ARAB appears over the wall. The ARAB climbs over and drops silently into the Courtyard. Behind the Reception, SPENCE moves very slightly as he raises his gun.

HAMID, *a small Arab, whistling, enters from the Archway leading off to the Kitchen. The* ARAB *hides behind the stairs.* HAMID *is quite unconcerned, crosses the Lounge, goes out into the Courtyard and through the Archway D.R. The* ARAB *comes out from behind the stairs, glances quickly towards where* HAMID *has gone.*

He takes out a long, curved knife and starts to climb the Stairs. SPENCE *rises out of the shadow of the Reception Desk, points his gun and fires. At the same time the* ARAB *at the top of the stairs turns and hurls the knife.* SPENCE *clutches at his chest, staggers a few paces out into the Lounge and falls to the floor with the knife protruding from his chest. The* ARAB, *who has been standing motionless at the top of the Stairs, now slowly falls across the Banisters and gently slides to the newel post at the bottom.*

After a moment of silence HAMID *returns through the Archway D.R. and still whistling. As he comes into the Lounge he switches on the lights, then crosses the room and goes flying over* SPENCE'S *body. He quickly picks himself up and looks around for an Assailant. He reacts to the body on the floor and then does an enormous 'Double Take' as he sees the body of the* ARAB *slumped across the Banisters. He dithers for a moment between the two bodies and finally lets out a cry)*

HAMID. Eloise! Eloise!
(ELOISE *hurries in from Archway L.)*

ELOISE. Whatever is it?
(ELOISE *looks at the bodies then she looks at* HAMID *who gives a terrified shrug.* ELOISE *moves over and looks at the body of* SPENCE)

It is Sir John Spence.

HAMID. So at last he has arrived. Lady Spence will be pleased.
(ELOISE *gives him a look and* HAMID *realises what he has said)*
Oh! Lady Spence will not be pleased!
(ELOISE *goes over to the body of the* ARAB)

ELOISE. Hamid, lift him up.

HAMID (*miserably*). Eloise—

ELOISE. Hurry! In a few minutes our guests will be expecting supper.

HAMID. Mohammed says I am permitted three lovely wives. And what do I end up with—one French dragon.

ELOISE. Vite!
(ELOISE *and* HAMID *lift the* ARAB. *His cloak falls to reveal an Army Uniform)*

ELOISE. A soldier.

HAMID. An Officer!

ELOISE. No—Do not touch either of them.
(ELOISE *goes upstairs.* HAMID *looks unhappily at the body*)

HAMID. On the very day our country has a military coup, what happens in our hotel? The young King hides here and two dead bodies turn up without booking.

ELOISE. Be quiet!
(ELOISE *gives the Code Knock on the Bedroom Door and* TRACY *open it.* ELOISE *stands to one side.* TRACY *comes out and* ELOISE *nods towards the Lounge.* TRACY *looks over the Banisters and takes in the scene below. Her face is expressionless. The* KING *takes a pace outside the Bedroom Door*)

KING. Lady Spence, look!

TRACY. Your Majesty! Please stay in your room.
(TRACY *comes down the Stairs followed by* ELOISE. TRACY *gives the dead* ARAB *a hasty glance as she passes and goes over to the body of* SPENCE. HAMID *is standing trembling beside it*)

HAMID. Poor Lady Spence. Dreadful. Your husband has been killed.

TRACY. Damned nuisance.

HAMID (*to* ELOISE). Her husband is killed and all she says is 'damned nuisance'.

ELOISE. Ssh! He wasn't really her husband.

HAMID. What do you mean?

ELOISE. They were secret agents working together on a forged passport.
(TRACY *has bent down and is going through his pockets. She takes his Wallet, Passport, Watch and Ring. Then she picks up his Gun*)

TRACY. That's right. I hardly knew him, really. He was a First Class Agent, I believe. Get rid of him immediately.
(TRACY *goes over to the body of the* ARAB)

ELOISE (*to* HAMID). Get rid of him, Hamid. In the cellar with him.

HAMID. I think I must have been drugged the day I married you.

ELOISE. You were. Now hurry. Vite!
(HAMID *drags the body of* SPENCE *off through Arch U.L.*)
You know this soldier?

TRACY. Yes. Captain Sareed el Dur. Military Intelligence.

ELOISE. Then the Military must be on to you.

TRACY. Not necessarily, but it does mean a delay.

ELOISE. You will still go through with it?

TRACY. Of course. But Spence must be replaced.

ELOISE. Can't you go through the Frontier Post without a husband? The young King is travelling as your schoolboy son, is he not?

TRACY. There has to be a Sir John Spence. The boy and I are travelling on Spence's phoney passport. We thought it would be safer that way.

(HAMID *returns from U.L.*)

HAMID. I have put Sir John in a barrel of wine.

ELOISE. Bon. Now get rid of the soldier.

HAMID. Oh, Allah, my wife treats me like a camel.

ELOISE. We are well paid by the British Government.

HAMID. *You* are well paid.
(HAMID *lifts the body of the soldier on to his back. There is the sound of a clanging bell from off R. They all freeze for a moment.* HAMID *with the body on his back.* TRACY *runs quickly to the Courtyard and looks over the wall*)

TRACY (*urgently but calmly*). Soldiers.
(HAMID *rushes around in circles with the dead body on his back*)

ELOISE. Hamid!
HAMID (*stopping*). What shall we do, Eloise? We will all be shot. I said it was too dangerous.

TRACY. Pull yourself together, Hamid. To the cellar with you.

HAMID (*moaning*). Ohh!
(HAMID *moves to the Arch L, as there is loud knocking from off L. They all freeze*)

ELOISE. They must have gone round to the back.
(*The Bell clangs from off R.*)

HAMID. We are surrounded!
(HAMID *rushes around in circles again*)

ELOISE. Tracy—the switch for the radio room.
(TRACY *hurries down to the stone seat and pulls out one of the stone 'roses'. This can now be seen to be a lever. She turns the lever*)

HAMID. Nothing is happening.

ELOISE. The electronic beam has not yet been broken.
(ELOISE *crosses the 'beam' which runs in a straight line from U.L.C. to D.L.C. and is about two feet above the ground. The Reception Desk revolves and the radio room comes into view. The bell clangs from off R. and the knocking is heard from off L.*)
(*to* HAMID). Put the soldier on the seat. Hurry.
(HAMID *sits the soldier on the Control seat. He pushes the head into a set of earphones which are attached to the control panel. This holds the body in place and makes it look as though he is listening to the radio.* ELOISE *is now on the revolve*)
See what they want, Hamid.
(*Exit* HAMID R.)

TRACY. Contact the major. Tell him we must have a replacement for Spence from Beirut.

ELOISE. What about the school uniform for the king?

TRACY. That's done. No one should recognise him.
(TRACY *crosses the beam and the revolve goes taking* ELOISE *and the body with it.* TRACY *switches off the lever on the stone seat. The shutters open and the* KING *leans out of the Bedroom window*)

KING. Are we not leaving, Lady Spence?
(TRACY *hurries upstairs*)

TRACY. A slight hold-up, your Majesty.

KING (*excited*). Has something gone wrong?

TRACY. No, nothing.
(TRACY *goes into the bedroom*)

KING (*half to himself—disappointed*). I thought it was going to be exciting.
(*The* KING *pulls his head back into the room.* HAMID *backs in nervously from R. followed by* CAPTAIN ABU *and an* ARAB SOLDIER)

HAMID (*backing in*). No, no, no, it is not convenient, Captain. Definitely . . .

(HAMID *looks quickly round the room, turning a circle. He is very agitated*)
If you could call back some other time.
(HAMID *remembers the Bedroom window and turns round to look at that. He is pleased to see that it is shut*)
Yes, yes. Call back some other time when everybody is out.

ABU (*curtly*). I wish to see the owner of the hotel.

HAMID. Yes, yes. Well here I am.

ABU (*refers to papers*). You are Madame Eloise Agazi?
  (HAMID *laughs*)

HAMID. No, no. That is my beloved wife. I am her wretched husband.

ABU. I wish to see Madame Eloise Agazi.

HAMID. You cannot, I'm afraid.

ABU. Why?

HAMID. She's in the wall . . . up the wall. We're all up the wall. The Military coup and everything, you know. I will tell her you called. Goodbye.
  (ABU *glares at him for a moment*)

ABU. I am Captain Abu, second-in-command, Frontier Security.

HAMID. Very nice.

ABU. Your hotel has been requisitioned for use of the military.

HAMID. Oh no! I mean, our unworthy hotel is not good enough for you, Captain.

ABU. On the contrary, it is ideally situated, being a mere hundred metres from the border. I will have a room overlooking the frontier post so that I may see the firing squad at work.

HAMID. F-firing squad?

ABU. For the Royalists.
  (HAMID *is only able to nod*)
Yes. There will be many members of the ex-government and supporters of the monarchy attempting to defect across the border there. None will slip through Captain Abu's net.
  (*There is the sound of banging from off L.*)
What is that?

HAMID. The back door - er - shall I see who it is?

ABU. Of course.

HAMID. Yes. Or perhaps I could wait here while you go and see who it is. No.
  (HAMID *hurries off L.* ABU *shakes his head wearily*)

ABU (*to* SOLDIER). Get my things from the truck.
  (ABU *exits U.R. as the radio room revolves with* ELOISE *and dead body on it.* TRACY *enters from bedroom*)

ELOISE. Oh Tracy. Our friend here makes it very difficult to operate the controls.
  (ELOISE *has alighted from the radio room and lays the soldier on the floor.* HAMID *enters from U.L.*)

HAMID. Eloise, will you please come at once.

ELOISE. But why?

HAMID. A gentleman from the British Consulate is in the bar.

ELOISE. Never mind. Now, take this man down to the cellar.

HAMID. How many barrels of wine do you think we've got down there?

ELOISE. Allez, allez.

TRACY. Hamid, what did the soldiers want?
   (ELOISE *operates switch to revolve radio room, and the Reception Desk comes round*)

HAMID. Oh, that is awful. The Captain has commandeered two bedrooms. You'd better get the King away in great haste, or very soon we will all be with Allah.

WOOLEY (*off-stage L.*). Madame Agàzi!
   (WOOLEY *enters from D.L. and walks briskly to C. without seeing* HAMID *and the body U.L.* ELOISE *opens the clock door and* HAMID *shoves the body inside.* WOOLEY *is a bald-headed pompous man in his fifties*)
   (*as he enters*). I'm not used to being kept waiting, Madame Agazi.
   (*The body going into the clock hits the chimes as the clock door is closed.* WOOLEY *turns as* HAMID *leans against the clock door*)
   (*to* ELOISE). Would you be Madame Agazi, by any chance?

ELOISE. Why, yes.

WOOLEY. Thank Goodness for that. Enchante. Très enchanté.

ELOISE. Lady Spence.

TRACY. How do you do.

WOOLEY. How do you do. Hubert Wooley of the British Consulate.

ELOISE. Can I help you?

WOOLEY. I sincerely hope so. I gather you have in residence a Mr. Fred Florence.

ELOISE. Yes, he's doing a turn in the local cabaret.

TRACY. Yes, I've seen him. Tells jokes and does a few impressions.

WOOLEY. Excellent. I have here a warrant for his arrest.

HAMID. His impressions are not that bad.

WOOLEY. The warrant is issued by the State Court but must be presented by the British Consulate.

HAMID. Oh, miserable M'Sieur Florence. What has he done?

WOOLEY. Oh, nothing. Apart from entering the country without a visa, working without a work permit and promising marriage to at least ten women in every country throughout the Middle-East.

HAMID. I am wondering what he could have accomplished with a work permit.

WOOLEY. Blighters like this, Lady Spence, give the old country a bad name. He'll be lucky if they don't execute him.
(*There is a crisp sound of the firing squad from off R. HAMID yells*)

TRACY (*looking out of window*). The firing squad.

WOOLEY. These fellows shoot first and ask questions afterwards.

HAMID. They don't bother to ask questions.

WOOLEY. Dreadful lot. Confiscated my car as well, damn it. I had to travel the last ten miles on the back of a camel; I shall never be the same again.

ELOISE. Oh, when M'sieur Florence is in court see if you can obtain for me my three months back rent. Room number ten, on the top floor.
(WOOLEY *moves to go upstairs and is stopped by* TRACY)

TRACY. Well, actually you've just this minute missed him. He's gone for a stroll. You'll catch him up in no time.

WOOLEY. Really, this is too bad. All this rushing about on an empty stomach. I'll be back as soon as I've seen this Florence fellow. I suppose I'd better stay the night, will that be all right?

ELOISE. Yes, most pleasant.

WOOLEY. And my camel?

HAMID. I'll get you a double room.
(*Exit* WOOLEY R.)

TRACY. Where actually is Mr. Florence?

ELOISE. Why do you want him?

TRACY. I believe Mr. Florence is our man.

ELOISE. Our man for what?

TRACY. For taking over as Sir John Spence.

ABU (*off*). Report to me when you get back.
(*Enter* ABU R.)

Madame Agazi?

ELOISE. Oui?

ABU. Captain Abu. I require one of the rooms overlooking the frontier post. What number will that be please?

ELOISE. Oh, Captain, I am so sorry, but all our rooms are already occupied.

ABU (*fiercely*). The number?

ELOISE. Room number eight.
(ABU *turns to* TRACY)

ABU. And what is your name, Madame?

TRACY. Lady Spence.

ABU. You are staying here?

TRACY. We're moving on tonight.

ABU. We?

TRACY (*after a moment's hesitation*). My husband, my son and myself. We understand the new military regime will not interfere with the free passage of British Nationals.

ABU. We will do our best to inconvenience you as little as possible, but until our heroic struggle against the decadent monarchy is finally won, there may be one or two minor annoyances for the traveller.

ELOISE. We thought the heroic struggle was already over.

ABU. Not until the Palace is ours and the King arrested.

TRACY (*casually*). And when might that be?
(ABU *smiles and exits R.*)

HAMID. It is madness to use M'sieur Florence. He is as stupid as I am.

TRACY. I quite agree, but Mr. Florence is our only hope. Eloise, this passport must be altered.
(TRACY *hands* ELOISE *Sir John's passport*)

ELOISE. Leave that to me. I am holding M'sieur Florence's trunk and also his passport in lieu of that back rent. It is simply a matter of a little forgery and exchanging the photographs. Hamid, come with me, please.
(ELOISE *exits U.L.*)

TRACY. No, Hamid. I'm going to get the King. You tell Mr. Florence I want to see him immediately.
(*Exit* TRACY *upstairs into bedroom*)

HAMID. What an unhappy situation. Dead bodies, variety artists, camels . . .
(FRED *enters from L.*)

FRED (*to* HAMID). That's it, I can get the bird in Scunthorpe—
I don't need it from the Arabs. I'm packing my bags.
  (FRED *moves upstairs*)

HAMID. You'd better be quick. Mr. Wooley from the British
Consulate is looking for you to arrest you.

FRED. I'm definitely packing my bags.
  (WOOLEY *has entered from R.*)

WOOLEY. Who are you?

FRED. What's it got to do with you?

WOOLEY. Do you know who I am?

FRED. No. Who are you?

WOOLEY. I'm Hubert Wooley of the British Consulate.

FRED. And do you know who I am?

WOOLEY. No.

FRED. Thank God for that.
  (FRED *jumps out of the window on the landing.* HAMID *yells and*
  WOOLEY *rushes out R. Almost immediately* FRED *returns half*
  unconscious being supported by WOOLEY *on one side and* CAPTAIN
  ABU *on the other. At the same time* TRACY *has opened the*
  bedroom window and seen HAMID *standing there*)

TRACY. Hamid, get that body out of there.
  (*She sees* ABU, WOOLEY *and* FRED *return*)
No, Hamid.
  (TRACY *closes window and enters from bedroom*)

ABU. I demand an explanation.

WOOLEY. I know no more than you do, Captain.
  (ELOISE *enters from U.L. and joins* HAMID, *who is fiddling with*
  the clock door, having just pushed the body back in there)

ABU (*to* FRED). What explanation have you for diving on to me
from a height of several metres?

WOOLEY. I have good reason to believe that this is the man I was
on my way to see. He answers the description of Florence.

ABU. Florence?

WOOLEY. Fred Florence, I have a court order for his arrest.

ABU (*letting go of* FRED). He attacked an officer of the new regime.

WOOLEY. Poppycock . . .!
  (WOOLEY *lets go of* FRED'S *other arm and* FRED *falls flat on his*
  face. TRACY *now hurries forward and kneels down by* FRED)

WOOLEY. . . . If this man is Fred Florence he leaves here with me.

ELOISE. This is my hotel and I will have peace and quiet.

ABU. You will all be placed under arrest.

HAMID. I knew everything would go wrong.

} All together

ABU. Silence, everyone, silence!
(*There is silence as* ABU *turns to* FRED, *whose head is now in* TRACY'S *lap*)
(*to* FRED). So—who are you and what is the meaning of your behaviour?

TRACY (*passionately*). Darling!
(TRACY *kisses him furiously.* WOOLEY *and* ABU *look at each other and back to the embracing couple.* FRED *comes out of the embrace looking delighted but bewildered. His face is close to* TRACY'S)

FRED. I've died and gone to heaven.

ABU. Answer me.
(FRED *goes to speak*)

TRACY. Darling!
(TRACY *embraces him again.* ABU *and* WOOLEY *exchange another glance.* WOOLEY *taps* FRED *on the shoulder.* FRED *looks up from the embrace*)

WOOLEY. Do you know this lady?

FRED. Who cares?
(FRED *quickly kisses* TRACY)

ABU. Will you answer me?

TRACY (*to* FRED). I think we'll go upstairs now, darling.

ABU. One moment. I take it you are - er - related to this lady?

FRED. You take it how you like, we're going upstairs now.

ABU. Halt. Come here, you.

TRACY. Captain, that's no way to address my husband.

FRED. Yes, that's no way — *husband*?

WOOLEY. I say! (*to* TRACY). This fellow is your husband?

TRACY. Naturally.

FRED. Naturally.
(FRED *cuddles* TRACY)

WOOLEY. Then you're not Fred Florence, a touring British Variety artist?

TRACY. Certainly not.

FRED. Certainly not.
(FRED *cuddles* TRACY *again*)

ABU. Whoever you are I see no reason for not placing you under close arrest.

TRACY (*sweetly*). You don't wish to make a silly mistake like that, Captain. This is my husband, Sir John Spence.

FRED. Yes—D.S.O., Y.M.C.A., F.F.I. and Bar. Have at you, sir (*to* TRACY). What next?

TRACY. Sir John is P.P.S. to the British Delegation at U.N.O.

FRED. That's right, P.P.S. to the U.N.O. Cry God for Harry . . .

WOOLEY. St. George for England.

FRED. St. Pancras for Scotland (*to* ABU). This chappie Florence, what's he been and gone and done?

WOOLEY. Enough to get himself ten years hard labour at least.

FRED (*to* ABU). That was clever. I never saw your lips move.

WOOLEY. That was me, Sir John.

FRED. Oh well, honi soit qui mal y asbestos, as we always say. To hell with you, I'm fireproof.
(*He laughs but neither* WOOLEY *nor* ABU *join in*)

ABU (*to* ELOISE). This man Florence is staying here?

ELOISE. That is correct, Captain.

ABU. Mm. I will see your hotel register.
(ABU *goes up to Reception Desk.* ELOISE *joins him*)

WOOLEY (*to* FRED). I still can't comprehend why you threw yourself out of the window.

FRED. The lift's out of order.

ABU (*with hotel register*). Yes, Fred Florence. Room number ten.

ELOISE. He's not in at the moment.

ABU. Who is this Stanley Charrington?

ELOISE. An oil prospector.

HAMID. But his prospects are not very good.

ELOISE. He's always drowning his sorrows.

ABU. And who is this in number 11?

ELOISE. Miss Farina Mahmoud, a friend of Mr. Florence. She is also appearing in the local night club.

HAMID. Farina is very sexy lady.

ELOISE. Hamid!

HAMID. She does the dance with the belly.
(HAMID *demonstrates this*)

ELOISE (*to* ABU). She will be down at the nightclub now.

HAMID. Doing her speciality with the tassles. One this way and one this way. Very lovely to behold.
(HAMID *demonstrates tassles revolving in opposite directions*)

ELOISE. Hamid!

FRED. And I might add, not easy to do. You see, the trick is—you have to get one going one way, the other the other way—and for an encore there's one underneath the arches and you're not sure which way that's going to go!

WOOLEY. Sir John!

FRED (*very posh again*). Did a bit of slumming while the wife was having a Turkish bath.

WOOLEY. It doesn't sound the sort of place a gentleman would be seen in.

FRED. I never saw anything but gentlemen. Beady-eyed, bald-headed, filthy-minded old . . . You weren't there were you?
(FRED *smiles at* WOOLEY *and pats his bald head. During the ensuing dialogue* ABU *and* ELOISE *continue to look through the register*)

WOOLEY. Certainly not. Now, if you'll excuse me I'll go to the club and find this Florence fellow.

TRACY. I think it is time we were on our way, darling.

FRED (*rubbing his hands*). You're dead keen to get upstairs, aren't you?

TRACY (*laughing*). No, darling. We're actually leaving tonight, remember?

FRED. Are we?

TRACY. You know we are (*to* WOOLEY). We're so looking forward to travelling through the night to Beirut.

FRED. I was rather looking forward to early morning tea and biscuits.

TRACY. Sir John can't do anything till he's had a cup of tea.

FRED (*with feeling*). Want a bet?

TRACY. Mr. Agazi, would you get our car from the garage, please?

FRED. Yes, get the Bentley. The ashtrays in the Rolls are dusty.

HAMID. What? Oh, yes.

(HAMID *takes a pace but stops*)
Nobody is to touch my grandfather clock. It has stopped and I do not want it started again.

(HAMID *hurries out through Arch U.L.*)

ABU. Yes. Everything appears to be in order.

TRACY. Then we may leave immediately, Captain?

ABU. You are in a hurry, Lady Spence.

TRACY. We must be in Beirut within 24 hours and it's a long journey by car.

ABU (*to* FRED). I fear your charming wife is determined to leave tonight.

FRED. I know.

ABU. You like it here?

FRED. I like it anywhere. Oh look, (*down front of* TRACY'S *dress*) red shoes.

ABU. You have a peculiarly British sense of humour, Sir John. Yes, you may go—after I have seen your passport.

FRED (*stops laughing*). Passport?

ABU. A mere formality.

FRED. A man in my position, Captain—the man from U.N.O. . . .

ABU (*sternly*). Your position is no different from anyone else's. Please remember that.

FRED. Of course, but - er - my passport is—

ELOISE. Your passport is here, Sir John.

(ELOISE *hands the passport to* FRED, *but* ABU *snatches it from her.*

While ABU *looks at the passport,* FRED *frantically mimes the fact that his own name and photograph will be in the passport.* ABU *looks up at* FRED, FRED *smiles at* ABU, *who returns to studying the passport.* FRED *continues to mime to* ELOISE)

ABU. It is in order.

FRED. I can explain everything . . . (*amazed*) . . . it is in order?

ABU. A very good likeness, your photograph.

FRED. Is it?

ABU. I see that you and your wife are travelling on one passport.

FRED (*blankly*). We are? We are. Are we?

ABU. Corps Diplomatic. What a splendid document this is. A key to so many doors. What - er - what are your wife's christian names?

FRED. I beg your pardon?

TRACY. Really, Captain, Elizabeth Jane—

ABU. Please!

FRED. Oh, I see what you mean. Elizabeth Jane.

ABU. Elizabeth Jane what?

FRED. No. Elizabeth Jane Spence.

ABU. Your wife has one more christian name.

FRED. Does she really?

ABU. What is it?
(TRACY *smells an imaginary 'Rose' on her bosom*)

FRED. Stinker? Buster? Titania? I don't know.

ABU. You don't know?

FRED. No. We've only been married two days.

ABU. Two days?

FRED. Yes. Been too busy to call her anything, really.

TRACY. Darling!

FRED. Elizabeth Jane didn't volunteer the information. I never thought to ask. Dash it all—we're on our honeymoon, aren't we?

ABU. Then what about your ten-year-old son?
(*There is a pause from* FRED)

FRED. Whose ten-year-old son?

TRACY. Yours.

FRED. Oh him! By my first wife! Shortly after the boy was born she left me for a Royal Army Service Corps Officer stationed at Blandford. My first wife's name was Augustine Harriet Amy Rosina Ivy. The Guards Officer was Thomas Arbuthnott Percival. . . .

ABU. Please!

FRED (*holding his eye*). Do you serve towels with your questions? (*wiping eye on* ABU'S *headgear*). Ah, so you do. How useful.

ABU. Excuse me.

FRED. Why, what have you done?

ABU. So, you are returning from your honeymoon with your ten-year-old son.

FRED. Roger.

ABU (*looks at passport*). That is correct, Roger. (FRED *looks surprised then grins*). Sir John, Lady Spence, bon voyage.

FRED. Suivez la piste.

ABU (*to* ELOISE). You will please come with me and allocate a room for Colonel Wazir.

ELOISE. Certainement.

(*Exit* ABU *and* ELOISE *upstairs*)

FRED. And the best of British luck with your revolt, old chap.

ABU (*stops on landing*). It is a military coup, Sir John. Not a revolt.

FRED. What's the difference, eh? You say you're having a military coup, and I say you're revolting.

(ABU, *for the first time, laughs, then realises and exits*)

Well, what about your real husband. Where's he?

TRACY. Oh yes. I'll have to tell you that won't I? I've left him.

FRED. Left him?

TRACY. Yes, it's sad. Drink. He hit the bottle very badly.

FRED. Oh, you poor thing.

TRACY. At this very moment he's probably up to here in wine.

(TRACY *indicates the top of her head*)

So you'll also be helping me, Mr. Florence. Much safer for Roger and me to leave the country accompanied by a man.

FRED. I suppose so.

TRACY. And from what I can gather you won't be sorry to get out of this place.

FRED. You're telling me! What with three months back rent, not to mention that tassle dancer down at the club.

TRACY. Miss Farina Mahmoud?

FRED. That's the one.

TRACY. You're not engaged to her, are you?

FRED. *I'm* not engaged to *her*, but in this country, if you're seen holding a girl's hand, they seem to think *she's* engaged to *you*!

TRACY. That's another good reason for you to leave.

(TRACY *opens her handbag*)

Right. There's Sir John Spence's driving licence, our plane tickets from Beirut to London—

FRED. I'm not altogether convinced that this is a good idea.

TRACY. —and £250.

FRED. I'm convinced.

(*The* KING *comes out on to landing. He is now dressed as an English schoolboy with his hair dyed blonde*)

KING. Excuse me.

TRACY. Please go back to your room, Roger.

KING. Are we not leaving?

TRACY. In a moment. This is your new Daddy.

FRED. Hello, son.

KING. You may kiss my hand.

FRED. I beg your pardon.

KING. And you may carry my suitcase back to my room.

FRED. Now let's get things straight, son. I'm not carrying your suitcase and I'm not kissing your grubby hand.

KING. Please do not raise your voice.

FRED. Raise my voice!—I'll smash your face in!

KING. I like you.

FRED. He likes me!

TRACY. Please, you must go back to your room.
(TRACY *goes up the stairs and pushes the* KING *to the bedroom door*)
(*to* FRED). We leave immediately.
(TRACY *and the* KING *exit into the bedroom*)

FRED (*counting money*). Five, ten, fifteen, twenty, twenty-five— (*he removes a note*) ten bob—how did that get in there? (*throws it away then picks it up again*). Keep that for tips.
.(*He is on his hands and knees as* FARINA *enters from arch R. She is dressed in a brief dancing outfit. She stands in front of* FRED. *He feels her shoes, then starts to feel her legs.*
He jumps up)

Farina! Farina, what the heck are you doing here?

FARINA (*in North Country accent*). Bloody-well looking for you, that's what.
(FRED '*shushes*' *her and looks round nervously*)

FRED. You'll have to get back to the club. I can't explain now.

FARINA. You'd better explain. What do you think you're playing at? Your act goes on in five minutes.

FRED. I'll be there in a moment. Has a fellow called Wooley been looking for me?

FARINA. I don't know—what are you doing with your trunk down here? You're doing a moonlight flit, aren't you?

FRED. Farina, you know me.

FARINA. I do that. You've done nowt but deceive me from the first moment we met. You said if I changed my name to Farina Mahmoud I'd earn a fortune as a belly dancer.

FRED. Well, you wouldn't have got very far if I'd come on the stage and said: 'And now, ladies and gentlemen, I want to introduce that lovely Egyptian belly-dancer, Edie Entwhistle'.

FARINA. There's nowt wrong with Edie Entwhistle.

FRED. In any case, I saved your bacon. You were over here with no money and no work permit, after being stranded with that Ice Show in Tel Aviv.

FARINA. It were an Ice Show in Cairo.

FRED. Well, wherever it was the whole damn lot melted, didn't it? Come on, I'll give you a kiss then you get back to the club.

(FRED *gives* FARINA *a peck on the lips, but she grabs him and embraces him passionately.* WOOLEY *hurries in angrily across the courtyard from R. He stops on seeing 'Sir John' embracing a belly dancer.* WOOLEY *coughs.* FRED *comes out of the embrace*)

Hullo there! Just signing a contract—Arabic style.

WOOLEY. A contract?

FRED. Yes. You can be a witness.

(FRED *kisses* WOOLEY *on his bald head*)

WOOLEY. Sir John, *please*!

FARINA. What flipping contract? And why are you talking with a plum in your mouth?

FRED. And this is Miss Farina Mahmoud.

WOOLEY. Oh, so you're the young lady who can—(*he repeats* HAMID'S *rotating business, but pulls himself up short*). I'm most terribly sorry.

FRED. Farina, this is Mr. Wooley from the—(*pointedly*) British Consulate.

FARINA. Oh, roll me over gently!

WOOLEY. She's not from the Middle East, is she?

FRED. Yes she learnt her English from a soldier—he was a York-shire Terrier!

(*Again* FRED *laughs. Again* WOOLEY *doesn't*)

WOOLEY. Sir John, I'm somewhat at a loss.

FARINA. What did he call you just then?

FRED. Quiet, Farina, or I won't put you under contract.

WOOLEY. What contract is this, Sir John?

FARINA. Sir John? You've gone stark raving bonkers.

(HAMID *enters from Arch R.*)

HAMID. Excuse me, Sir John, but your car is ready.

FARINA. *Car*?'.

HAMID (*noticing* FARINA). Oh, hell!—Eloise!

(HAMID *rushes to stairs as* ELOISE *enters on landing*)

FARINA. So you *are* scarpering, you big twit.

ELOISE. Farina, you should be down at the club.

FARINA. I'm not budging.

(TRACY *hurries out of the bedroom with the* KING)

TRACY. Come on, Roger.

KING (*calling down to* FRED). We're ready, Daddy.

FARINA. Daddy!?

FRED. Oh Gawd!

FARINA. Just a minute—
(*Suddenly there is the sound of very nearby Sten-gun fire from off R., and some shouting in Arabic.* HAMID, *who is by the landing window, drops to his knees and looks out*)

HAMID. Soldiers! Chasing two men!
(*There is the sound of the engine starting, more gunfire and more shouting. Everybody starts to rush at once except* FRED *and* FARINA)

TRACY. Take the boy back to the bedroom.
(TRACY *runs downstairs and exits R.* ELOISE *and* KING *exit into bedroom.* STAN *runs downstairs, followed by* ABU *who exits R.* WOOLEY *also exits R.*)

HAMID (*to* FRED). Do not let anyone touch my clock!

ABU. Guard! Guard!

FRED. They went that way.

STAN. Charge. (STAN *follows* HAMID *off R.*)

FARINA. Come on then, who's the bird with the big charlies.

FRED. Sssssssh.

FARINA. Who is she?

FRED. She—she's a woman.

FARINA. I could tell it wasn't Godfrey Winn.

FRED. She's my agent and personal manager.

FARINA. Get lost.

FRED. It's true.

FARINA. Yes. About as true as I'm riding this bicycle. And what about that little boy up there, who's he?

FRED. That's not a little boy, that's Jimmy Clitheroe.

FARINA. I didn't come up yesterday, you know.

FRED. I'm only playing it cagey because of Wooley.

FARINA. Wooley?

FRED. He's got enough on me to keep me in jail here for the next twenty years.

FARINA. That I can believe.

FRED. So you get back to the club and I'll be along as soon as I've sorted it out.

FARINA. All right, then—but kiss me first.

FRED. God, I'm weak.

(FARINA *flings herself into his arms.* WOOLEY *hurries into the Courtyard and stops on seeing* FRED *and* FARINA *in a warm embrace. They come out of it.* FRED *sees* WOOLEY *and smiles at him*)

WOOLEY. Sir John!

FRED (*going Etonian again*). Had to initial a couple of clauses in the contract. Farina, why don't you do old Woolbags here a big favour?

FARINA. I beg your pardon?

FRED. As you know Mr. Florence so well you might have some idea where he might be laying low.

FARINA (*not comprehending*). Laying low?

FRED. Yes. Probably some café you and he frequent at the *other* end of the town somewhere.
(FRED *indicates off L.*)

FARINA. Oh, I see! Yes. I know the very place. Come, Mr. Wooley, I will show you the way.

WOOLEY. Will you really? I mean - I - er . . . Won't you catch cold running around like that?

FARINA. Of course not.

FRED (*to* WOOLEY). If she wants to talk about contracts watch the small print on the bottom.
(*Exit* WOOLEY *after* FARINA *D.L. Enter* TRACY *R.*)
Well, are we off?

TRACY. We can't go, we've no car.
(ELOISE *enters from bedroom*)

ELOISE. Why, what happened?

TRACY. Our car's just been smashed to pieces. Two political prisoners crashed it trying to get across the border. Captain Abu's just suggested that we take the inter-continental train to Beirut; and that leaves at seven a.m. tomorrow morning.

FRED. Well, I suppose we'd better turn in and make the best of it. Tea for two at 5.15, Eloise.

(FRED *moves upstairs*)

TRACY. We'll have to tell him, Eloise.

ELOISE. I agree. We have no time to waste. I'll ask Beirut to get a helicopter over here.

FRED. Helicopter? What's the rush?
(ELOISE *pulls out the switch on the stone seat for the radio-room and* TRACY *crosses beam*)

TRACY. Tell them we want it immediately.

FRED. You got relations in B.O.A.C. or something?
(TRACY *moves to beam.*

TRACY *crosses through the beam and the Reception Desk revolves.*

FRED *looks down and then looks up in disbelief at the radio room*)
Have you got a licence for that thing?
(ELOISE *goes into the radioroom.* TRACY *walks through the beam and the piece revolves again*)
What's going on?

TRACY. The mechanism is operated from here by this switch. When it is out you have to break the electronic beam, which is projected through the wall in a straight line here.
(TRACY *switches the lever off*)

FRED. Electronic beam, helicopters . . .

TRACY. You've got to be told, I'm afraid.

FRED. Thanks very much.

TRACY. Mr. Florence, can you imagine what Madame Agazi is doing in there?
(FRED *goes to speak, but decides against it*)
She is contacting M.I.6.

FRED. M.I.6?

TRACY. Overseas British Intelligence.

FRED. You mean that's what . . .? (*indicating revolve*).

TRACY. Yes.

FRED. And that's why . . .? (*indicating switch on stone seat*).

TRACY. Yes.

FRED. And that's who . . .? (*indicating bedroom*).

TRACY. Yes.

FRED. Don't call me, I'll call you.
(FRED *rushes upstairs*)

TRACY. Mr. Florence!
(FRED *stops*)
Shall I tell you why you've got to see this thing through.

FRED. I don't care why.

TRACY. This country's future depends on you.

FRED. Then it's going to get into one hell of a mess.
(FRED *moves again*)

· TRACY. Fred. England expects . . .

FRED. I know. That's why they call it the mother country.

TRACY. Listen. That boy we're taking across the border, do you know who he is?

FRED. As far I'm concerned, he's Jimmy Clitheroe.

TRACY. He's the King.
(FRED *slides down the stairs on his heels and supports himself at the bottom around the post*)

FRED. The King?
(FRED *rushes upstairs again*)

TRACY. That boy's life is in your hands.

FRED. Why pick on me? Why not use Stan Charrington?—After all, he's English.
(FRED *moves to go*)

TRACY. You know he drinks all day and is permanently plastered. No, it must be you.

FRED. It's got nothing to do with me. Why didn't M.I.6 supply one of your agents to be Sir John Spence?

TRACY. They did. He's in the cellar with a knife in his chest.
(FRED *slides down the stairs to the bottom again*)

FRED (*gulping*). He's dead?

TRACY. In a barrel of Beaujolais.

FRED. I see what you mean when you said your husband had taken to drink.

TRACY. Yes, I'm sorry about that, Mr. Florence.

FRED. Hey, wait a minute. If they've killed your agent—they must be on to you.

TRACY. I don't think so. The man who killed our agent is dead himself.
(FRED *nods dumbly*)

FRED. Where is he?

TRACY. In the grandfather clock.
(FRED *bangs against the clock. The Reception Desk revolves half open and* ELOISE *appears with it*)

ELOISE. Oh Tracy, the major wants to talk to you. He's worried about Mr. Florence being brought in on this.

FRED. He's worried?!

TRACY. All right.
(TRACY *join* ELOISE *on the revolve.* ELOISE *pulls a large switch on the revolve and it starts to move*)
(*to* FRED). Keep an eye on things.

FRED. Well, don't leave me here.

ELOISE. We won't be long.
(*The revolve has turned and the Reception Desk is back in position. FRED looks at the clock and frowns. He goes over to it and surveys it. He opens the door a fraction and peeps inside. STANLEY CHARRINGTON enters from the Arch R. He wears khaki shorts and jacket, and is as drunk as always*)

STAN. Hullo, there!
(*FRED, in his fright, steps into the clock and, amid much chiming, immediately steps out again. He stands with his back to the clock looking terrified*)
Something wrong?
(*FRED shakes his head*)
You feeling all right?
(*FRED nods his head*)
By God, you're talkative, aren't you?
(*FRED shakes his head*)
Why aren't you down at the club, Fred?

FRED. Club, what are you talking about—club! I'm afraid I haven't the faintest notion what you're referring to.

STAN (*after a moment to collect his thoughts*). What are you talking like that for, Fred?

FRED. Fred, my name's not Fred, I happen to be Sir John Spence, one of Her Majesty's Arabian Knights.
(*STAN takes a swig from his hip-flask*)

STAN. Aren't you my old friend, Fred Florence?

FRED. Never heard of the chappie.
(*STAN feels FRED'S face and then sits on the stool of the Reception Desk*)

STAN. Quite amazing. I suppose I'm still who I think I am.

FRED. I really wouldn't know. I've never set eyes on you before today.

STAN. No, of course you wouldn't if you're not Fred Florence. He's a very good friend of mine.

FRED. Really?

STAN. Yes, a very good friend. Charrington is my name. Stanley Charrington. I'm a guest in this hotel, and a life-long searcher after the thick black stuff.

FRED. Thick black stuff? What's that—syrup of figs?
STAN (*chuckling*). Syrup of figs! That's very funny and very moving too! No. Oil. I search after oil and although I've not as yet struck a gusher, I live in hopes. Cheers.

FRED. I suggest you go to bed for a couple of days.

STAN. I don't want to go to bed. Are you absolutely positive you're not Fred Florence?

FRED. Definitely! I have a passport to prove it.
(*The clock door gently opens and the body of the dead* ARAB *is seen standing inside.* FRED *hasn't seen this but* STAN *does a very slow 'Double Take' as his bleary eyes take in the picture.* FRED *continues to talk as* STAN *moves up to the clock and surveys the dead* ARAB)
John Spence is the name. Sir John Spence. My wife and I came here for a little peace and quiet and I can only assume that you have mistaken me for someone else, but I can assure you that I am Sir John Spence and that I hold an extremely important position representing Her Majesty's Government at the United Nations.
(*Enter* HAMID *U.L. He closes the clock door locking* STAN *in*)

HAMID. I said nobody was to touch my grandfather clock.
(*Exit* HAMID *R.* STAN *starts banging on the inside of the clock door.* FRED *hastily lets him out.*)

STAN. I thought somebody shoved the lights out (*to* FRED). That fellow in there, is he a friend of yours? You're not leaving him in there are you? He was a ghastly colour and a messy drinker, too—Dubonnet all down the front of his jacket. He's a soldier, isn't he?

FRED. I wouldn't know. Why don't you go to bed?

STAN (*struggling*). I don't want to go to bed. Are you sure you're not Fred?
(ABU *enters from Arch R. very briskly*)

ABU. Are you still up, Sir John?

FRED (*putting on the posh*). Oh, yes, still up, skipper.

STAN. You must be who you say you are. (*to* ABU). He looks so much like . . .
(FRED, *to cover up, lets out a scream.* STAN *and* ABU *look at him*)

FRED. Ah! (*he pinches* STAN'S *bottom to stop him saying any more*).
(STAN *jumps*)

ABU (*to* STAN). Who are you, sir?

STAN. Stanley Charrington.

ABU. Captain Abu. The hotel has been requisitioned for use of the military.

STAN. Damn cheek. I suppose that drunken soldier is something to do with you, is he?

FRED. Ah! (*he pinches* STAN'S *bottom again*).

ABU. Drunken soldier?

STAN. Yes, the one in the . . .

FRED. Ah! (*he pinches* STAN'S *bottom again*).

ABU. Drunken soldier?

STAN. Yes, the one in the . . .

FRED. Ah! (*he pinches* STAN'S *bottom again*).

STAN. Has everyone gone mad round here?

ABU. Sir John, please (*to* STAN). Are you saying that one of my men is intoxicated?

STAN. Oh, you mean . . .

FRED. Ah!
(STAN, *confused pinches* ABU'S *bottom*)

FRED. (*hastily walking* ABU *away from* STAN). The poor *fellow* doesn't know what he's saying, Captain.

ABU. If one of my men has been drinking, Sir John . . .

FRED (*as they go*). No, no, no. It's transference of the guilt complex. Obviously Mr. Charrington likes the old - er - (*he mimes drinking*)—and so he thinks that everyone else is drunk while he's sober. The more sober they are the more drunk he *thinks* they are. And the drunker he gets the more sober he thinks he is. I'll look after him, don't you worry.

(FRED *propels* ABU *off R.*)

STAN. That was very interesting, what you were saying, old boy. Do you know I couldn't understand one word of it.
(*The window of the bedroom opens and the* KING *pops his head out*)

KING. Is everything all right?

FRED. Get back in there, you little horror.

KING (*laughing*). I think you're very funny.
(*The* KING *withdraws his head and closes the window*)

STAN. Who is that?

FRED (*after a slight pause*). Jimmy Clitheroe.

STAN (*after another pause*). I think I will go and have a drink.
(STAN *gets on stool behind desk*)
(*into phone*). Hello, get me Rome, Vat 69.
(*The revolve starts turning and* ELOISE *appears as* STAN *disappears*)

FRED (*to* ELOISE). Charrington's turned up.

ELOISE. Get rid of him.

WAZIR. Sir John, you are very energetic.

FRED. I'm the athletic type. Having my nightly practice. Standing high jump.
(FRED *does a couple of 'Arms Stretch'*)

WAZIR. Will you join me in a drink?

FRED. Thank you.
(FRED *is looking nervously at the Reception Desk*)

WAZIR (*to* HAMID). Two scotches on the rocks. Very British drink, is that not so?

FRED. I really think you'd enjoy your drink more standing up.

HAMID. Oh, no, Sir John. Sitting down more pleasant.
(FRED *looks furiously at him and points frantically to the Reception Desk.* WAZIR *catches this and* FRED *goes into a few more 'Arms Stretch'.* HAMID *hands them their drinks and pushes the trolley L. through the beam.* FRED *has followed him quickly, and the Reception Desk revolves a fraction and then returns.* FRED *jumps over the beam and returns to* WAZIR. WAZIR *is beginning to worry about 'Sir John's' leaps.*

HAMID *returns through the beam and the Reception Desk revolves.* FRED *rushes past* HAMID *and through the beam, returning the Reception Desk.* HAMID *and* WAZIR *look at each other.* HAMID *shrugs.* FRED *goes to jump over the beam, but realises it is becoming exhausting, so crawls under it.* HAMID *and* WAZIR *are now looking very perplexed*)

WAZIR (*to* HAMID). My Second-in-Command has arrived?

HAMID. Captain Abu? Oh yes, sir.

WAZIR. Very good. If you will organise a little supper for me I shall retire to bed. Oh, get me a plaster for my foot.

HAMID. Yes, sir.
(HAMID *goes to walk through the beam, but* FRED *lifts him by his collar and trousers and heaves him up and over the beam, and he exits through Arch U.L.* WAZIR *looks at* FRED *in amazement*)

WAZIR. Practising again?

FRED. Yes, just strengthening the shoulder for putting the shot (*he demonstrates*).

WAZIR. You are certainly a fanatic.

FRED. Yes, I run the United Nations Health and Beauty Club.

WAZIR. Is that a fact?

FRED. I do wish you'd go upstairs and put your blister to bed.
(CAPTAIN ABU *enters from D.R. across the Courtyard*)

ABU. Ah!

FRED (*immediately puts his hands up*). I don't know your wife!

ABU. Good evening, Colonel.

WAZIR. Captain Abu, all is well?

ABU. Excellent. We have already executed three escapees. Still not in bed, Sir John?

FRED. No, not yet. Still up and about.

WAZIR. He has been practising his athletics. Amazing fellow. You will have a drink, Captain?

ABU. I wish to discuss my defence plan.
(*ABU starts walking upstage keeping the beam between himself and FRED. They walk back downstage. ABU flicks his military cane nearly across the beam. FRED is terrified in case it actually crosses it*)

WAZIR. You will have a drink first. Waiter. You will be delighted with the news from the Capital. The Military have taken over Government House and the Royal Palace will soon be ours.

ABU. Excellent (*he walks forward*). Now for the frontier security.
(*FRED is so relieved that ABU did not cross the beam, that he forgets and crosses it himself*)

WAZIR. We have also under our command the radio and television stations.
(*The Reception Desk revolves and FRED runs through the beam again to close it. He then jumps over the beam to join ABU and WAZIR*)

ABU. These are the defence measures I have taken.
(*Enter HAMID U.L.
As he walks through the beam the Reception Desk starts revolving. FRED runs through the beam and bangs into the clock. The clock doors opens revealing the dead body. HAMID sees him and rushes through the beam again, opening the revolve as he does so. He closes the clock door and stands there as FRED breaks the beam once again to close the revolve. He returns to the desk*)

WAZIR. Waiter, fetch the drinks trolley.

FRED. I'll get it.
(*He waves away HAMID who exits U.L. FRED then jumps over the beam, grabs the trolley, wheels it through the beam, thus opening the revolve. He then closes the revolve by breaking the beam with his leg, like kicking a door closed with your back to it*)

FRED. Would you like a splash?
(*He squirts the soda syphon at WAZIR'S leg, having handed ABU and WAZIR a drink. WAZIR jumps up and FRED is able to get to the switch and push it in. He lies back exhausted as the curtain falls*).

CURTAIN
END OF ACT ONE

ACT TWO

TIME: Half an hour later.

WOOLEY *is speaking on the telephone.*

WOOLEY (*on phone*). Yes . . . Yes, I quite understand, Sir Humphrey. Who . . .? Miss Farina Mahmoud? . . . Oh no, I won't let her out of my sight. Her performance starts in a few minutes and I can assure you, I shan't take my eyes off her . . .
(*He twirls a pencil round and round, with a tassel at the end. Embarrassed, he stops*)
No . . . No . . . Thank you Sir. . . . Yes. Goodbye!

(WOOLEY *puts the phone down. He rubs his hands with pleasure and then checks on the time by looking at the grandfather clock. He frowns and checks with his own watch. He decides that the clock is slow, so goes to alter the hands. As he does so* HAMID *enters, sees* WOOLEY *with his clock and yells*)

HAMID. Ah!

WOOLEY (*nearly collapsing*). Ah!! (*seeing that it is* HAMID). What the devil did you yell like that for?

HAMID. Did I yell?

WOOLEY (*running his hand over his bald head*). Made my hair stand on end.

HAMID. You were touching my clock.

WOOLEY. What? Oh yes. It happens to be nearly an hour slow.

HAMID. That is correct. I prefer it to be one hour slow. Then I can get up one hour late every morning.

(WOOLEY *exits, trying to work this out.* HAMID *gives a quick look around and then opens the clock door. He starts to lift the body out as* ABU *and* WAZIR *enter through landing arch.* WAZIR *is holding a golf club in his hand*)

WAZIR. You have done well, Captain.

ABU. Thank you, Colonel.
(HAMID *jumps and shoves the body back into the clock. In doing so he catches his fingers in the clock door. He yells and stands there sucking his fingers.* ABU *and* WAZIR *watch him from the balcony*)
What are you doing?

HAMID (*dusting clock*). I was dusting my clock. I can dust my clock if I want to. I love my clock as much as I love my wife. (*kisses clock*). Mmm. Better than my wife.
(HAMID *moves to go*)

ABU. Come here you.
(HAMID *stops, worried*)
Where are our suppers?

HAMID. A thousand pardons, Captain.

ABU. I will have mine in my room. I have some reports to study. Colonel?

WAZIR. No. I will eat in the dining room. And I would like a carafe of red wine, please.

HAMID. The Beaujolais?

WAZIR. If it is full-bodied.

HAMID. Oh, yes!
(HAMID *chuckles and exits U.L.*)

WAZIR. This is the life, eh, Captain? Good hotel, good food, and a beautiful red wine.

ABU. Yes, sir. Now, if you will excuse me, I will check the frontier post.

WAZIR. Good idea. And tell the driver of my motor car that I shall be making a tour of the post immediately I've dined.

ABU. Don't you think, Colonel . . .?

WAZIR. No, I do not think. Do you know why the General has seen fit to put me in charge of this sector?

ABU. The General is your father.

WAZIR. Exactly. And if there are any slip-ups, do you know what will happen?

ABU. The General will blame me.

WAZIR. Exactly. Carry on.

ABU. But . . .

WAZIR. Carry on!
(ABU *sighs and exits R.*
WAZIR *puts the golf club under his arm like a cane and exits through the landing arch.* HAMID'S *head appears round L. Arch.* ELOISE *pushes him on and enters after him.* ELOISE *opens clock door*)

ELOISE. Vite. To the cellar with him.

HAMID. But the soldiers' suppers . . .

ELOISE. Do that as well.
(HAMID *exits U.L. with the* BODY *over his shoulders. The bedroom window opens and* TRACY *and* KING *lean out*)

TRACY. Eloise!

ELOISE. Oui?

TRACY. Where's Mr. Florence?

ELOISE. In his room recovering from the shock you gave him.

TRACY. Get him. We're ready to leave.

ELOISE. But, with your car out of action . . .

TRACY. I have a plan.

KING. Poor M'sieur Florence. He will faint when he hears it.

TRACY. Ssh! (*to* ELOISE). Don't waste any time.
(TRACY *shuts the shutters.* ELOISE *moves towards the stairs, as from off* FRED *and* STAN *are heard singing. They enter down the stairs clutching each other and singing drunkenly*)

ELOISE. Sir John, I thought you were in your room.

FRED. I was going back to my room when I ran into my good friend here, and he invited me into his room for a large Scotch.
(STAN *giggles*)

STAN. Hello, Eloise.

ELOISE (*to* FRED). I think it would be unwise for you to see your "*wife*" in that condition.

FRED. I tell you, one more drink and I'd be through that door like a dose of salts.
(FRED *and* STAN *giggle.*
FRED *goes into a fit of laughter*)

ELOISE (*whispers urgently*). You fool! Have you no sense at all? There is that girl in there risking her life. I'm disappointed in you.

FRED. I didn't want to get involved . . .

ELOISE. And maybe that girl didn't want to get involved, but you are—both of you. Now pull yourself together. Vite. You must be prepared to go at any time. (*to* STAN). M'sieur, you are very naughty, getting Sir John drunk.

STAN. To tell you the truth I didn't realise it was Sir John at first. I thought it was my old friend, Fred Florence.

FRED. Poor Fred.

ELOISE (*to* STAN). You do not know what or who you are seeing half the time. Your blood is full of alchohol.

STAN. Well it keeps the mosquitoes away.
(STAN *makes a drunken zig-zag movement with his hand.* FRED *and* STAN *giggle.* ELOISE *throws her arms in the air with disgust*)

ELOISE (*going upstairs*). Lady Spence will be very angry when I tell her of this.

FRED. You're a sneak, Eloise.
(ELOISE *exits bedroom.* STAN *starts to stagger backwards away from* FRED)

STAN. I want to ask you a very important question, and don't move away when I'm talking to you. Are you positive you're not Fred Florence?
(FRED *shakes his head sadly*)

FRED. Fred Florence is no more.
(FRED *drinks*)

STAN. No more, Sir John?

FRED. Gone, never to return.

STAN. Gone? What a dreadful thing. How long has he been gone.

FRED. He's been gone some time now.

STAN. Well, then he should be nearly there by now. Cheers

FRED. Cheers.

STAN. I remember him well.

FRED. Who?

STAN. Fred Florence.

FRED. What did you say his name was?

STAN. Who?

FRED. Fred Florence.

STAN. Never heard of him.

FRED. You mean the fellow who reminded you of me?

STAN. Yes. Though now I come to scan your countenance, there's not much similarity. (*he peers closely*). No. He was a man of the theatre. Many a time and oft I have sat in the local night club watching Fred Florence perform—God, he was dreadful. But what a heart. He had a heart as big as my liver.

FRED. That's quite a heart. Tell me, do you like drinking?

STAN. Not really, Sir John.

FRED. Well, why do you do it.

STAN. It passes the time away while I'm getting pickled.

FRED. Why don't you join Alcoholics Anonymous?

STAN. Sir, I have my own society.

FRED. What's that?

STAN. Alcoholics Unanimous.

FRED. How does that work?

STAN. I'll tell you. When a fellow feels like giving up drink, he gets me on the telephone, and I talk him out of it. (*spills drink down trousers*). Now look what I've done. I've wet myself. Never mind, I don't think it's an inside job.

FRED. I like you. (*he holds* STAN'S *hand*)

STAN. I like me too. Somebody said you were on your honeymoon, Sir John. (FRED *laughs*). Is that funny?

FRED. Hilarious.

STAN. You did say you were on your honeymoon?
(FRED *nods*)
Then why are you holding my hand?
(*Pause*)

FRED. My wife doesn't love me.

STAN. Oh.
(*They drink*)

FRED. And she's absolutely lovely, too.

STAN. Absolutely.

FRED. But she doesn't love me.

STAN. She's mad.

FRED. Maybe I'm not as lovely as she is.

STAN. You are. You are.
(*They drink*)
Lovely girl, your wife.

FRED. Are you married?

STAN. Yes, sir, I am wed. My wife's an angel.

FRED. Really?

STAN. Well, the sooner the better.
(TRACY *enters from bedroom followed by* ELOISE *who exits R.* ELOISE *hurries down to* FRED)

TRACY (*angrily to* FRED). How could you?!

FRED. I did it to forget.

TRACY. Forget what?

FRED. I've forgotten. You?!

STAN. I think I'll get ready for my midnight drilling in the desert . . .

FRED. But the night is young yet, Stanley.

STAN. No, no, Livingstone, I feel lucky tonight. Maybe I'll strike a gusher of gas in the North Sea.

FRED. But the North Sea is 6,000 miles from here.

STAN. I know, but I'm doing it the hard way.
(STAN *exits upstairs*)

TRACY. You fool!

FRED. Funny. That's what Eloise said. I think it must be carried unanimously.

TRACY. In our business, Mr. Florence, you need a cool head and a clear brain.

FRED. Well, I'm not in your business.

TRACY. Yes you are. Right up to your neck. So pull yourself together.

FRED. I'm afraid I'm going to say goodbye. 'Bye, 'bye!

TRACY. Oh no you're not. You know too much, Mr. Florence. You're not going anywhere.

FRED. Who's going to stop me?
(TRACY *lifts up her skirt to reveal a suspender-belt armoury complete with guns, knives, hand grenades, etc.*)
I've heard of chastity belts, but this is ridiculous!

TRACY. Now listen. I've thought of a way of getting out of here, but you've got to sober up. (*takes something from ring*). Here, take this. It's a pill.

FRED. A pill? It's not one of those, is it? That wouldn't do me much good, would it; it might be the wrong day. And then there'd be a pregnant pause!
(TRACY *pushes pill into* FRED'S *mouth as he laughs at his joke*)
Where's the enemy. I'll take 'em single handed.

TRACY. Good. Now listen—neither London nor Beirut can help us until morning. By then it may be too late.

FRED. Roger!
TRACY. So, I've got a plan.
FRED. Good show.
TRACY. We can be safely across the border within half-an-hour.
FRED. Good show.
TRACY. All you've got to do is steal Colonel Wazir's car.
FRED. Good night! Those pills don't last long do they?
TRACY. The car's outside. We only have to deal with the driver.

FRED. Deal with him?

TRACY (*taking earring off*). This earring dissolves in liquid.

FRED. Who's your jeweller? Timothy White's?

TRACY. Any more questions?

FRED. Yes. Why the Colonel's car in the first place?

TRACY. It's now the only car in the village.

FRED. They'll recognise it as the Colonel's at the border post.

TRACY. Of course. That's why Colonel Wazir has to 'phone them at the post and tell them that he has loaned his car to Sir John Spence.

FRED. Oh—and the Colonel will do that little favour, will he?

TRACY. Of course not. Somebody has to ring up the border post pretending to be Colonel Wazir.

FRED. What idiot are you going to get to do that?
(FRED *laughs, but suddenly shudders*)
Oh no. I'm not cut out for this secret service stuff. Lying, cheating, killing, it's against my religion. I'm a devout coward. I could get killed.
(TRACY *goes upstairs*)

TRACY. We'll worry about that when the time comes.

FRED. I want to worry about it now! It's all very well for you with Woolwich Arsenal tucked under your skirt.

TRACY. I've got something for you, too.
(TRACY *exits upstairs to the bedroom*)

FRED. If she thinks I'm going to wear a loaded kilt she's out of her mind.
(TRACY *comes out of the bedroom carrying a suitcase*)

TRACY. Come along, Mr. Florence. You'll have to help me with this—it's very heavy. And be careful. There are weapons in there, not play-things.
(TRACY *hands* FRED *the case, which* FRED *places on the stone seat and opens*)
Now, this fountain-pen. Only use it in a tight corner.

FRED. What do I do—write to my M.P.?

TRACY. You push the nib out, jab it into your assailant's skin, and he'll be unconscious in three seconds.

FRED. A poison-pen!

TRACY. Exactly, so be careful with it.
(FRED *puts it in his pocket.* TRACY *takes a cigar and lighter out of the case*)
Now this cigar and lighter are in case we get separated and you want to contact me.

FRED. What do I do—send up smoke signals?

TRACY. The cigar is an aerial and direction-finder. You stick it in your ear. To transmit, you operate the lighter so. To receive you release and listen; got it?

FRED (*taking lighter and sticking cigar in ear*). Hallo there, I'm receiving you loud and clear.
  (TRACY *takes out a large children's book of "Snow White"*)

TRACY. Here's your code-book. By the way, don't mention any proper names. My code-name is Snow White and yours will be . . .

FRED. Don't tell me—Dopey. I can see him sitting there . . .

TRACY. Precisely. Here's your toilet-bag.
FRED. My favourite soap, how did you guess. You'll be a little lovelier each day, with fabulous pink Camay . . . (*throws soap in air*).

TRACY. The soap's a hand grenade!

FRED. Oh!
  (*He just catches the soap*)

TRACY. The talcum-powder's lethal gas, and the deodorant . . .

FRED. Stink bomb?

TRACY. Cyanide.

FRED. What's the toothbrush for?

TRACY. Cleaning your teeth.

FRED. Ask a silly question . . .

TRACY. The pipe is a tape-recorder, the cigarettes are distress signals.

FRED. Of course. What's this?
  (*He takes out a yellow folded up dinghy*)

TRACY. A self-inflating dinghy.
  (FRED *spreads it on the stone seat*)

FRED. That should come in handy in the middle of the desert.

TRACY. Mr. Florence, we have to be prepared for all eventualities. Now this is the most important thing of all.

FRED. What's that?

TRACY. That contains your suicide-pill.

FRED. You must be joking! Bye, bye! It's been a lot of laughs.
  (FRED *turns and runs to Arch L. and bumps into* HAMID, *who has entered carrying two trays.* FRED *ends up with one of the trays as he passes* HAMID)

HAMID (*taking tray*). Thank you.

TRACY. Who are those trays for, Hamid?

HAMID. Captain Abu and the driver. Colonel Wazir is taking his in the dining room.

TRACY (*taking tray*). I'll take the driver's to him.

HAMID. Thank you. Most kind.
(HAMID *exits upstairs*)

TRACY. Looks appetising.
(TRACY *drops an earring into wine glass on tray*)

FRED. That's nothing permanent, is it?

TRACY. No, it'll keep him quiet for a while.

WAZIR (*off*). Yes, thank you. I'm going down to the dining room.

TRACY. Get rid of that suitcase.

WAZIR (*off*). Did you remember my wine?

HAMID (*off*). Yes, sir.

WAZIR (*off*). Very good.

(FRED *throws the suitcase off-stage and* TRACY *exits D.R. as* WAZIR *enters from Archway.* WAZIR *has a tennis racquet with him, and swishes it as he comes downstairs.* FRED *sees that the dinghy is still on the stone seat. He quickly sits on top of it*)
Ah, Sir John! It's a hell of a racket you British are making.

FRED (*whispering*). Most sorry, old chap.

WAZIR. I'm about to go into supper, Sir John. Will you join me?

FRED. No, no. I think I'll just sit here.

WAZIR. Well, will you join me in a drink?

FRED. No, I'd rather sit here.

WAZIR. Then I'll join you.

FRED. I shouldn't do that if I were you.
(FRED *spreads himself over the dinghy and sets the self-inflating mechanism off. A loud hissing noise is heard*)

WAZIR. What is that?

FRED. What is what?

WAZIR. That noise like wind.

FRED. Wind?
(*The dinghy underneath* FRED *starts to inflate and, to* WAZIR'S *amazement,* FRED *rises*)

WAZIR. Yes, is it you?

FRED. Certainly not. Is it you?

WAZIR. No.
(*The dinghy is now obviously inflated*)
Where have you gone?

FRED. I've gone with the wind. Why don't you go and have your meal before your soup gets cold and your curry goes out.

WAZIR. Yes, I think I will.
(WAZIR *turns to go but turns back when,* FRED, *in a desperate effort to keep the dinghy down, falls off the seat. He quickly clambers back on and lies full length.* FRED *can no longer cope with the expanding dinghy and falls off again, taking the dinghy with him and ending up underneath*)
(*amazed*). What is it you are doing?

FRED. That's a good question. (*gets to his feet and holds up dinghy*). Yes, I remember now. I was just taking this soapdish up to the bedroom.

WAZIR. Soapdish?

FRED. Yes. The wife and I will have a little game with it before turning in.

WAZIR. Game?

FRED. Yes—marvellous! We chase one another around it and whoever gets caught first . . .

WAZIR. Yes?

FRED. Has to pay a forfeit.

WAZIR. What's the forfeit?

FRED. Depends on how tired you are after chasing round. Bon appetit!

WAZIR (*perplexed*). Salaam. Very energetic, these British.
(*By this time* FRED *has exited R. and* WAZIR *D.L. There is a loud bang, off R., and a few seconds later* FRED *enters looking dazed and clutching a scrap of yellow rubber.* WOOLEY *enters U.L.*)

WOOLEY. Was that you, Sir John?

FRED. No, now listen, Wooley. I want to have a chat with you. We must leave right away.

WOOLEY. Leave?

FRED. Yes. Just you and I.

WOOLEY. I don't understand. What about your wife?

FRED. Mr. Wooley, I'd never met my wife until tonight.

WOOLEY. Never . . .?

FRED. Never!

WOOLEY. But you have a little boy, haven't you?

FRED. He's not my little boy. He's not even my wife's little boy.

WOOLEY. Well, who is he?

FRED. It's not *who* is he, it's *what* is he.

WOOLEY. I think you've made it very clear what he is!

FRED. He's the King.

WOOLEY. The King? What about Lady Spence . . .?

FRED. Lady Spence! That's not Lady Spence, that's Snow White. And do you know what she wants me to do? She wants me to stick a cigar in my ear and call myself Dopey. You must put me safely away somewhere.

WOOLEY. Yes, yes, of course. I'll help all I can. You relax. It was that fall from the window, I expect, Sir John.

FRED. Wooley, at this moment Sir John Spence is in the cellar.

WOOLEY. What's he doing down there?

FRED. What do you think he's doing! He's floating in a barrel of Beaujolais.

WOOLEY (*startled*). Floating in a barrel of Beaujolais . . .! What is that thing you keep waving at me, Sir John? (*he points to the yellow remnant of the dinghy*).

FRED. That's a rubber dinghy, of course!
  (WOOLEY *hesitates and then starts to walk nonchalantly towards the Courtyard.* FRED *rushes after him D.R.C.*)

Mr. Wooley, I'll have to admit it—you want me.
WOOLEY (*nervously*). No, I don't think so, thank you.

FRED. Yes. I'm the man you're after. I'm Fred Florence.

WOOLEY. Yes, I see. Er—how long have you been Fred Florence?

FRED. You don't believe me, do you?

WOOLEY (*backing away*). Yes, yes. I'm sure you have papers, passport . . .

FRED. Of course not. I've got Spence's passport.

WOOLEY. Naturally. He won't need it if he's travelling home in Beaujolais. (WOOLEY *laughs foolishly*)

FRED. I'm Fred Florence, I tell you. Look—impressions! I'm Fred Florence, I tell you. Look, I do impressions. I do James Cagney and Norman Wisdom . . .

WOOLEY. Very nice for them, I'm sure.

(FRED *gets wig etc. from his trunk which has been D.L. since beginning*)

FRED. But I always start with this one. Long John Silver. Ha, ha, Jim lad. Ha, ha . . . (FRED *throws the wig etc. back into the trunk*). James Cagney. You dirty rat, I'm going to beat you yet . . . (*he slaps* WOOLEY'S *face—sings*). I'm a Yankee doodle dandy—

(FRED *dances back to trunk and takes out a cap, which he puts on*)

Norman Wisdom. (*singing*). Don't laugh at me 'cos I'm a fool . . . (*Throws cap back into trunk*)

But, I always finish with a song. A song entitled "When I fall through the mattress, I'll see you in the Spring", and then I go off . . . Now, I don't care if you put me away for twenty-five years, as long as I don't have to impersonate Colonel Wazir on the telephone.

WOOLEY. You want to be Colonel Wazir as well?

FRED. I don't want to be anybody, but it's that woman. That Snow White. And if I told you what she has in her knickers you'd never believe me . . .

WOOLEY. Take it easy, Sir John, take it easy!

FRED. You've got to get me to the Consulate!

WOOLEY. Let's wait until the morning . . .

FRED (*grabbing* WOOLEY *desperately*). Wooley, I need you! I need you.

WOOLEY. Put me down, please!

FRED. You don't believe me. All right, all right, I'll show you something else.

(FRED *goes to the clock*)
The man responsible for Sir John Spence's death, . . .

WOOLEY. Oh, Sir John is dead, is he?

FRED. What else would he be doing in a barrel of Beaujolais.

WOOLEY. Quite, quite.

FRED. The man responsible for Sir John's death is in this clock.

WOOLEY (*nodding*). I see. Now how long has he been in there?

FRED. Ever since he was killed.

WOOLEY. Oh, he's also dead, is he?

FRED. Of course. What else . . .

WOOLEY.

FRED. } . . . would he be doing in a grandfather clock?

FRED. You think I'm crazy.
(FRED *dramatically opens the clock door towards himself, masking for him the fact that the clock is empty.* WOOLEY *surveys the empty clock*)
Now are you convinced?

WOOLEY (*pointedly*). Definitely!
(FRED *closes the door*)

FRED. Then let's go.

WOOLEY. Just a moment. We have no transport.

FRED. What about your camel?

WOOLEY. He's got the hump. Er . . . he's fast asleep in the stable.

FRED. Well, let's go and wake it up.
(TRACY *has entered from D.R. She is standing there holding a gun.* ELOISE *is behind her*)

TRACY. Mr. Wooley.

WOOLEY. Ah, thank heavens, Lady Spence.
(TRACY *squeezes the trigger. There is a jet of white smoke from the gun into* WOOLEY'S *face.* WOOLEY *gives an inane giggle and collapses to the ground*)

FRED. You've killed him. She's killed him.

ELOISE. I'll get Hamid.

TRACY. Right.
(ELOISE *exits U.L.*)

FRED. You've killed him. What did you have to kill him for?

TRACY. I didn't kill him. This is a Smith and Wesson Paralysing gun.

FRED. Smith and Whosit whatsit?

TRACY. That puff of smoke will temporarily destroy the co-ordination of his complete nervous system. We will be across the border before he regains consciousness.
(TRACY *lifts up her skirt to put the revolver away*)

FRED. I wish you'd stop doing that!
(TRACY *picks up the 'phone and listens*)

TRACY. You were very foolish to ask Wooley for help.

FRED. I'm no good to you. Honestly, cowards run in our family.

TRACY. The Colonel's car is outside, Mr. Florence. The driver won't bother anyone for several hours. All you've got to do is telephone them at the frontier post and say you're Colonel Wazir. (*on 'phone*). Operator? This is the hotel El Nirvana. Could you put me through to the frontier post . . .

FRED. I don't even know Colonel Wazir.

TRACY. You do impersonations, don't you?

FRED. Yes, but I've never been shot for doing a bad one.

TRACY (*on 'phone*). Frontier post? I have Colonel Wazir for you.
    (TRACY *thrusts the 'phone into* FRED'S *hand*)

FRED. I refuse to be Colonel Wazir.

    (TRACY *lifts her skirt*)

(*on 'phone*). Colonel Wazir here! What? . . . Hello? Speak in English. Yes, we must all speak English . . . Yes, for when we invade Great Britain later in the year . . . You did not know that? Well, you don't know everything do you? Now listen. I am loaning my motor car to a very important Englishman. Sir John Spence. He is travelling with his wife and son. You let them through, understand? . . . Yes their papers are all in order, I checked them myself . . . you'll recognise him . . . extremely handsome fellow. And Lady Spence has two big beautiful-er-suitcases . . . Yes. And their son is a little boy . . . Goodbye. God bless Mohammed . . . God bless Mohammed . . . God bless Mohammed!

    (FRED *puts 'phone down and collapses*)

TRACY. Who was that?

FRED. Cassius Clay's manager, I think.
    (ELOISE *hurries in from Arch L. followed by* HAMID)

ELOISE. Quickly, Hamid, get rid of him!
    (HAMID *takes* FRED *under the arms and starts to move him*)

FRED. Not me, you fool!

TRACY. No, Hamid, Mr. Wooley!

WOOLEY (*getting up*). Ah, Lady Spence . . . (TRACY *shoots him again*). Oh, she's done it again . . . (*goes to clock which* HAMID *opens for him*). Going down! Sports-ware. (*gaily*). Straight thro' the knicker department.

    (WOOLEY *sinks down in the clock and* HAMID *shuts clock door. Phone rings.* ELOISE *picks up the phone and speaks with false gaiety*)

ELOISE. Good evening. Hotel El Nirvana . . . Captain Abu? (*hesitating*). I am not certain . . . Oh . . . Oh, I see. One moment.
    (ELOISE *covers the mouthpiece*)

It is the General himself, wishing to speak to Captain Abu. He is telephoning from the Palace, and has discovered the King is missing.

TRACY. We can't let the news get to Abu until we've crossed the frontier.
 (TRACY *takes the 'phone from* ELOISE *and speaks into it*)
 (*on 'phone*). Captain Abu for you.
 (TRACY *holds the 'phone to* FRED. FRED *furiously shakes his head, then stops. He indicates for* TRACY *to lift her skirt. She does so*)

FRED (*on 'phone. In high-pitched sing-song voice*). Captain Abu . . . English . . . (*he shrugs to* TRACY). Talking Arabic . . . (*on 'phone*). Mm-mm-mm . . . (*to* TRACY). Keeps saying "Khalifah".

ELOISE. Khalifah!

TRACY. What does that mean?

ELOISE. The King!
 (TRACY *and* FRED *react to this*)

TRACY (*to* FRED). Keep him talking.

FRED. Can't stop him. (*on 'phone*). Mm-mm-Khalifah . . . Khalifah . . . Mm . . .
 (WAZIR *enters from Arch D.L. with a table napkin tucked in his collar. He stops on seeing* FRED *at the 'phone.* ELOISE *and* HAMID *mask* WOOLEY'S *body, which is behind the basket.* TRACY *coughs to attract* FRED'S *attention*)
 (*on 'phone*). Khalifah . . . Khalifah . . . Khalifah . . . (FRED *sees*

WAZIR. *On 'phone. Weakly*). Khalifah, one Khalifah . . . (*brightly*) two beetroot and a pound of Brussel sprouts. Thank you. Goodbye. God bless Mohammed.
 (*Puts the 'phone down. To* WAZIR)
 What would we do without Sainsbury's?
 (WAZIR *smiles politely, not understanding*)

WAZIR (*to* FRED). Sir John, perhaps Lady Spence and yourself will join me for an after-dinner drink.

FRED (*easing* WAZIR *to Arch D.L.*). Topping, old boy, absolutely spiffing.

WAZIR. Brandy, Claret, Port?

FRED. I'll have the same. (*to* TRACY). Do something!
 (*Exit* FRED *and* WAZIR *off L.* FARINA *enters from Arch R.*)

FARINA. Where's my Fred?

ELOISE. Shush.

FARINA. I'll not shush. I want to know what's going on.

TRACY (*to* FARINA). I suggest you keep out of this.

FARINA. You can belt up, for a start. That fellow Wooley reckons he's going to have me deported.

TRACY. We'll discuss it later.

FARINA. We'll discuss it now.

TRACY. Will you please be quiet.

ELOISE. Go back to the club, girl. Out, out, out!

FARINA. All right, all right, all right. Don't get your knickers in a twist.

TRACY. Will you please leave.

FARINA. I will not! I'm not budging from this spot till I've seen my friend Fred and found out what's going on.
(TRACY *has taken a syringe from under her skirt and stuck it into* FARINA'S *backside*)
What have you done?
(TRACY *shows her the syringe*)

TRACY. It's only temporary. You will come to no harm.

FARINA. No harm? She's jabbed my bum! Look.
(HAMID *goes to look, but* ELOISE *restrains him.* FARINA'S *arms start to go rigid in front of her. After a moment her whole body is stiff*)

TRACY. All right, Hamid. You can help me pick her up now. Which is her room?
(HAMID *and* TRACY *pick* FARINA *up like a plank of wood*)

ELOISE. Upstairs. Room number eleven.

ABU (*off*). Madam Agazi! Madame Agazi!

ELOISE. Captain Abu. Vite!

TRACY. The cellar.
(HAMID *and* TRACY *hurry off U.L. carrying* FARINA *between them.* ABU *enters R.* HAMID *enters U.L. and starts dusting the clock*)

ABU. Madame, your hotel is like a market-place. Who was screaming just now?

ELOISE. Screaming?

ABU. Screaming.

ELOISE. My husband.
(HAMID *gives her an outraged look*)

ABU. It sounded like a woman's voice.
(ELOISE *shrugs and gestures to* HAMID. ABU *goes across to* HAMID. HAMID *dusts*)
You were screaming?

WAZIR. Very much so.
(FRED *sees* TRACY *and the* KING *come out on to the landing.* FRED *puts his arm round* WAZIR *and talks to him, while* TRACY *and the* KING *tiptoe down the stairs and exit R.*)

FRED. Then you must come to our country. Our country is the greatest pudding country in the world. We have treacle pudding, college pudding, bread-and-butter pudding, cabinet pudding . . . We even have clubs named after them.

WAZIR. Well, perhaps you could make me a member of the pudding club.

FRED. No, I think that might be a little difficult . . . But I must be off now.

WAZIR. Are we not having a drink together?

FRED. No, I must go for my nightly constitutional. Twice round the Sphynx and back in time for cocoa!
(FRED *exits R.*)

WAZIR. Amazing fellow.
(*The clock door opens.* WOOLEY *staggers out*)

WOOLEY. Good evening.

WAZIR (*astonished*). What are you doing in there?

WOOLEY. In where?

WAZIR. In the grandfather clock.

WOOLEY. Oh, I sleep there.

WAZIR (*to* ELOISE). There are many things which need to be explained in your hotel.

WOOLEY (*to* WAZIR). I've got pins and needles up my nose and I feel most peculiar, Snow White. You don't mind my calling you Snow White, do you? You see, I know what you have up your knickers.

WAZIR. What's the matter with everybody here?

WOOLEY. Do you know that feeling when you are floating on air.
(WOOLEY *'floats' around the room.* WAZIR *watches him in amazement*)
It must have been that gun that did it.

WAZIR. Gun, what gun?

WOOLEY. I don't know. White Tornado. Delicious.

WAZIR (*to* ELOISE). Who is this man?

ELOISE. I don't know. I will get Hamid to remove him.
(ELOISE *hurries off U.L.*)

WOOLEY. My legs are made of rubber. Boing! boing! boing!
(WOOLEY *bounces to and fro*)
Oh I wish she'd shoot me again.

WAZIR. Shoot you? Who shot you?

WOOLEY. I don't know. She's all sorts of people. And so is he.
You see. They're escaping.

WAZIR. Escaping? Who is escaping?

WOOLEY. The two Jimmys. Clitheroe and Cagney—you see they're
spies.

WAZIR. Spies?

WOOLEY. Mince pies.
(WOOLEY *giggles and starts to pinch himself all over*)

WAZIR. Who are you, sir?

WOOLEY. No trick questions, please.

WAZIR. You are English, yes?

WOOLEY. No. My mother was a Welsh Rabbit, and my father a
Scotch Egg.

WAZIR. Who are you?!

WOOLEY. A Manchester Tart. Yes, of course, I must be Florence.

WAZIR. Florence?

WOOLEY. Florence of Arabia. Fred Florence. The scoundrel, the
night club entertainer—the impressionist!
(WOOLEY *opens the trunk and puts on Long John Silver hat*)
Ha-ha, Jim lad, Ha-ha!
(WOOLEY *hops to and fro*)
Ahoy in front, and avast behind!
(WOOLEY *puts tri-corn hat back in trunk, and grabs cap which
he puts on*)
Norman Cagney. You dirty rat! "I'm a Yanky Doodle Dandy"
Jimmy Wisdom . . . "Don't laugh at me, 'cos I'm a fool . . ." But, I
always finish with my latest song; If you knew Suzie as I knew her
mother, her father would be after you too.
(WOOLEY *dances off through the Arch U.L. and immediately
returns dancing with* ELOISE. HAMID *follows them in and taps*
WOOLEY *on the shoulder.* WOOLEY *bows to* ELOISE *and starts
dancing with* HAMID. *This is brought to a halt by a tremendous
explosion off D.R.* WAZIR *hesitates and then rushes off R.* ABU
hurries on from the landing)

ABU. Colonel! Sergeant! Turn out the Guards!
(ABU *exits through Arch R.*)

WOOLEY. Wait for me.
(WOOLEY *bounces off after him*)

HAMID (*chuckling*). What a beautiful bang. Did you hear it, Eloise?

ELOISE. Of course I heard it. What was it?

HAMID. You don't know. But I do. Oh, yes. I deal with the Military.

ELOISE. What are you talking about?

HAMID. I fix them fine.

ELOISE. What have you done?

HAMID. I, the worm, I have turned.

ELOISE. What have you done?

HAMID. I put a bomb in Colonel Wazir's car.
(ELOISE *is horrified*)

ELOISE. Idiot.

HAMID. Idiot?
(FRED *staggers in through the Courtyard holding* KING'S *hand.* FRED *is very dishevelled and his face's is grimy. He is glowering. The* KING *starts to laugh*)

FRED. What's so funny?

KING. You are. You came straight through the roof. Whoosh!
(*The* BOY *makes an arc with his hand*)

FRED (*gasping*). There was a bomb in the engine.

ELOISE. Yes, we know.

HAMID (*trying to be gay*). I expect someone thought it a good idea to explode the Colonel's car.

FRED. What fool could have thought that?

HAMID (*laughing*). Me.

ELOISE. Where is Lady Spence.

KING. Ah, she is very brave, Madame.

ELOISE. She is all right?

KING. After the bang the road is filled with soldiers. The lady tell the funny man and me to hurry back here and hide while she lead the soldiers off.

HAMID. A decoy. She is brave.

ELOISE (*pointedly at* FRED). Yes. She has courage.

FRED. I'd have courage if I was wearing her bloomers.

ELOISE. She will have gone to our second rendevzous. The cafe in the square. I will go to her. And you, your Majesty, we must now hide you safely away. Hamid, the beam.
(HAMID *operates the beam*)

KING. What are you doing, Madame.

ELOISE. The bedrooms are too dangerous now. This switch controls the door from inside, you'll be safe in there.
(ELOISE *crosses the beam. The section revolves*)

KING. You are all very kind, Madame.

ELOISE. Poor little boy. You two remain here. And be on your guard should the Colonel return. (*to* FRED). Here. Shoot to kill.
(ELOISE *hands him a gun and exits.* FRED *and* HAMID *look at each other.* HAMID *smiles*)

FRED. I should use this on you.
(HAMID *smiles and shakes his head*)

HAMID. Oh, you are too kind.

FRED. I don't know how I ever got caught up in this.

HAMID. No, I am not knowing either.

FRED. Would you say spying was dangerous?

HAMID. All right. Spying is dangerous.

FRED. You're an idiot.

HAMID. Yes that is true. Do you know, I am renowned as the most useless person in the whole of the village.

FRED. You can say that again.

HAMID. All right, I am renowned as the most . . .

FRED. D'you know what I like about you, Hamid? It's nice to know that there's somebody else in this world who's as stupid as I am.

HAMID. Oh, pleased to meet you.

FRED. Hamid, I'm not cut out for this.

HAMID. I am not, either.

FRED. I'm so useless, I might be doing everybody a favour by just walking away.

HAMID. I know a place in the desert about twenty kilometres from here where we could hide.

FRED. What about transport?

HAMID. Mr. Wooley's camel is outside.

FRED. What about food?

HAMID. Oh, the camel isn't hungry. (*realising what* FRED *means*). Oh, that is already there.

FRED. What about money?

HAMID. I know a little old lady in the village who makes money.

FRED. Counterfeit?

HAMID. Oh yes, she's got two.

FRED. Right, let's go.
(FRED *and* HAMID *start to move as section revolves and the* KING *appears*)

KING. Excuse me . . .! I don't want you to think I am a cissy, but I am a bit frightened in there.

FRED. Try and go to sleep.

KING. I get bad dreams.
(FRED *and* HAMID *start to go in as a red light starts to flash furiously on the indicator board*)

FRED. What's that mean?

HAMID. I do not know.
(*The light stops flashing*)

VOICE (*from speaker*). 'Are you receiving me? Come in Snow White. This is Grumpy'.

FRED. I know what that is. How do you work this thing?

HAMID. I have not any idea.

VOICE (*from speaker*). 'Are you receiving me? This is Grumpy to Snow White. Over'.

FRED. We've got to speak to him.

VOICE (*from speaker*). 'Come in, Snow White! Come in'.

FRED (*shouting*). We'd come if we could, you twit!
(FRED *switches a switch*)

ANNOUNCER. 'This is the B.C.C. Light Programme'.

VOICE. 'This is Beirut . . . Beirut to El Nirvana. Is everything going according to plan?'

FRED. No, it isn't!
(HAMID *switches a switch*)

VOICE (*in French*). 'Et maintenant nous continuerons le concert avec une selection'.
(*The* KING *switches a switch*)

VOICE. 'When asked his view on national opinion polls he replied—'.
(*As* FRED *turns a knob there is a raspberry-like atmosphere noise from the radio*)

VOICE. 'Mirror, mirror on the wall, who is the fairest . . ."
(*Noel Coward is heard singing 'Someday I'll find you'. A switch is turned and the volume suddenly goes very loud.*
The Beatles are heard singing 'Yeah, Yeah, Yeah!' STAN *appears on the landing with a bottle of brandy*)

STAN. What the hell's going on?
(STAN *comes downstairs.* FRED *bundles the* KING *and* HAMID *into the radio room and revolves it out of sight. 'Yeah, Yeah, Yeah!' is still heard coming from the wall.* FRED *hurries to* STAN *and starts to push him back upstairs*)
Where's the music coming from?

FRED. What music?
(*The music stops*)

STAN. I could have sworn I heard music.
(*Bing Crosby singing 'White Christmas' is heard.* STAN *looks at* FRED. *The music stops.* ABU *appears D.R.*)

ABU. Sir John.
(FRED *slips down the stairs on his heels, in surprise*)

FRED. Hello, there.
(STAN *attempts to come downstairs on his heels and falls into* FRED'S *arms*)

ABU. Sir John, I wish to speak to you immediately.

FRED. Of course, Captain. Let's go upstairs.

ABU (*angrily*). The Colonel's car has just been blown to pieces.

FRED. No!

ABU. Yes—and I have received a report that you were seen in the vicinity at the time.

FRED. Ridiculous!
(*The 'phone rings.* ABU *storms over to it and picks it up. He moves away to C. with the 'phone, as* FRED *rushes to answer it*)

ABU (*on 'phone*). I'll get that . . . Captain Abu speaking.
(*Bing Crosby is heard singing 'White Christmas'*)
(*on 'phone*). What? I can't hear . . .

(FRED *rushes around behind him and leans on the Reception Desk.* ABU *turns to* FRED, *who mouths to* 'White Christmas'. STAN *comes down and gazes at* FRED)

ABU. (*shouting to* FRED). Be quiet!

(*The singing continues, so* FRED *can only shake his head and continue to mime*)

(*shouting louder*). Shut up!

(*The music stops and* FRED *smiles apologetically at* ABU. ABU *returns to the 'phone and moves further to the centre of the Lounge*)

(*on 'phone*). Now, what are you saying? . . . The General . . . Yes, I am listening . . .

(*The Beatles singing* 'Yeah, Yeah, Yeah!' *start to blare out.* ABU *turns furiously to* FRED, *who is now miming to them.* STAN *is intrigued and joins in.* FRED *is furiously, but surreptitiously tapping on the panel, while* ABU *is trying to carry on the 'phone conversation.* 'Yeah, Yeah, Yeah' *goes into Chinese music.* STAN *and* FRED *are miming making these strange noises. The music suddenly stops.* FRED *and* STAN *are left holding their noses and tapping their throats. They emit a few weak final Chinese noises.* STAN *is thoroughly enjoying the game. He pulls up his trousers and moves upstage, doing a little dance by himself*)

Sir John, shut up! What do you take me for? (*raspberry noise from radio room—on 'phone*). What? Khalifah . . .? The King? . . . this is the first time I've heard about the King . . .

(FRED *has taken out the gun given him earlier by* ELOISE *and advances on* ABU. *The music suddenly starts again. It is now the Beverley Sisters singing* 'Sisters'. ABU *turns sharply and* FRED *puts the gun away.* FRED *grabs* STAN *and they go into miming* 'Sisters'. ABU *is still attempting to get information from the telephone call.* ABU *turns and* FRED *mimes playing the Reception Desk as an organ as Reginald Dixon is heard playing* 'I do like to be beside the seaside')

(*on 'phone*). Never mind. Tell me about the King . . .

(FRED *finishes miming, and pulls out the telephone connections*)

(*on 'phone*). Hullo! Hullo!

(WOOLEY *'bounces' in from the Courtyard still suffering from lack of co-ordination in his muscles*)

WOOLEY. Hullo!

ABU. Be quiet!

(*The music stops*)

WOOLEY (*to* FRED). You're the man from the Consulate, and I want to run away with you.

STAN. What's the next number?

(FARINA *hurries in from the Arch D.L. clutching her bottom*)

FARINA. Where's my Fred? Ah, there you are.

ABU. Everybody shut up!
(*There is silence as he goes back to the 'phone. Suddenly the music starts again. This time it is the Black and White Minstrels singing 'California, here I come'.* ABU *turns on them.* FRED *and* STAN *take* WOOLEY *and* FARINA *and go into a song and dance to 'California'.* FRED *leads them upstairs*)

(*pressing receiver up and down*). Hullo! Hullo!
(FRED *steps aside and* WOOLEY *and* FARINA *disappear down the landing.* FRED *does a frenzied side-step shuffle and goes flying through the landing window*)

THE CURTAIN FALLS

END OF ACT TWO

ACT THREE

Time: Fifteen minutes later.

The Theatrical Basket is no longer on the stage. ABU *is speaking on the telephone.* HAMID *and* ELOISE *are standing together having been questioned by* ABU.

ABU. Yes, General . . . no, General . . . yes. General, I have explained it was not I to whom you were speaking on that occasion . . . I do not know . . . The last time? No, Sir, it was not a party . . . Yes, I know there was singing . . . a raving English lunatic . . .

    (WAZIR *enters cheerfully down the stairs with a squash racquet*)
. . . yes, General . . . no, General . . . but I can assure you, General, but General . . .

WAZIR. Is that the General?

ABU (*to* WAZIR). Yes, Sir.

WAZIR. I'll take it.

ABU (*sighing*). Yes, sir. (*into 'phone*). Colonel Wazir would like to speak to you, sir.
    (WAZIR *takes the 'phone.* ABU *crosses and glares at* HAMID *and* ELOISE)

WAZIR (*on 'phone*). Acting Colonel Akmed Pasha Kubla Ali Baligaza Wazir speaking . . . Hullo, Daddy . . . how are you? . . . Good. And all my Mummies are well? . . . as I am understanding it, Captain Abu was having some kind of a party . . . (ABU *reacts to this*) . . . and this eccentric Englishman was singing and then he danced out of the window . . . I did not see it but it must have been very humourous . . . (*he laughs inanely again*) . . . No, I cannot question him . . . he's in bed with concussion . . . No, Papa—with concussion . . . you have my personal assurance that since I arrived no one has crossed the border . . . the King? If he is in the vicinity, he shall be flushed out! . . . Pardon? . . . which one? I believe that was "Oh, I do like to be beside the seaside". Yes, Papa, I'll try and get a copy for you . . . It was just a suggestion . . . yes . . . but . . . of course I realise that I am not here to play games . . . you have my personal . . . (*to* ABU) . . . he just rang off.

    (WAZIR *puts the squash racquet on the 'phone instead of the receiver.* ABU *corrects it*)
The General was not pleased.

HAMID. He enjoyed "Beside the Seaside". Yes?

WAZIR. Oh, yes.

ABU. With respect, Sir, that is not the point. Someone in this hotel has been impersonating Officers of the new Regime. Namely, myself and Colonel Wazir. Why—eh?

ELOISE. We do not know.

WAZIR. And who has been blowing up my motor car?

HAMID. The children around here are very playful.

WAZIR. It appears there is much to be done, Captain Abu.

ABU. Yes, sir.

WAZIR. I shall go and er - er -

ABU. Lie down?

WAZIR. What a good idea. I must have my wits about me to-morrow. Good night.
(WAZIR *goes up the stairs singing "Beside the Seaside". He exits. ABU glares at* HAMID *and* ELOISE)

ABU. Now!
(HAMID *jumps*)
You will not find me so lenient as the Colonel. I am not happy with things in this hotel.

HAMID. We gave you the bridal suite—

ABU. Quiet! We have learnt that the King has escaped from the Capital.

ELOISE. Down with the monarchy—pigs!
(ELOISE *spits and* HAMID *gets it in the eye*)

ABU. And I am wondering if there is any connection between the King's escape and the impersonation of myself on the 'phone. Could it have been one of the guests or—(ABU *leans close to* HAMID)—yourselves, perhaps!

ELOISE. M'sieu, anyone could have come into the hotel and used the telephone.

ABU. Mm—possibly. But there are other strange occurrences in this hotel that need explaining. Sir John Spence up there—

HAMID. Now, he *is* having a screw loose—

ABU. Be quiet!

HAMID. Be quiet!

ABU. A nobleman from Great Britain—dancing, singing, jumping out of windows in the middle of the night.

ELOISE. He is on his honeymoon.

ABU. So! I never knew anyone behave like that on their honeymoon. (*to* HAMID). Did you jump out of a window on your wedding night?

(HAMID *looks at* ELOISE)

HAMID. No, I was pushed.

ABU. And Lady Spence? Where is she? Disappeared. Vanished on her honeymoon.

HAMID. Maybe she has gone back to mother.

(ABU *glares at him*)

ABU. And maybe she is the woman seen running away from Colonel Wazir's exploded motor car. Now why should Lady Spence be running away from Colonel Wazir's exploded motor car? (*to* HAMID *quickly*). Shut up!

ELOISE. You do not know it was Lady Spence. It could have been anyone.

ABU. Lady Spence is not in the hotel.

ELOISE. Out walking possibly. She will return. She is leaving with her family in the morning.

ABU. No, Madame. No one is crossing the border until I have interrogated them—passport or no passport. In the meantime no one is to leave the Hotel. You two are confined to your bedroom. (*They both hurry through Arch L.* ABU *looks around the room. He stops by the clock, hesitates and then looks inside. It is empty.* ABU *exits D.R. singing "White Christmas". After a moment the bedroom door opens and* FRED'S *head appears. It has a bandage around it. He comes quietly down the stairs carrying a suitcase. He is obviously scarpering. He starts to tip-toe towards the courtyard. The Reception Desk starts to revolve.* FRED *hides as the young King comes out of the Radio Room. The Reception Desk revolves back into place. The King starts to tip-toe towards the courtyard,* FRED *steps down behind him and taps him on the shoulder. The King jumps and turns on* FRED *with a knife in his hand*)

FRED. Hey, what have you got behind your back. A knife? What are you doing with a knife? Where do you think you're going?

KING. I am going to cross the border by myself.

FRED. You're going to do what?

KING. I have caused the English Lady enough trouble.

FRED (*reassuring*). She's alright. She's in this house in the village arranging to get us safely away.

KING. She will not succeed. It is too dangerous now with the whole army looking for me. You see, I must try.

FRED. How will you get across the border.

KING. I will steal Mr. Wooley's camel.

FRED. But they'll recognise you at the border post.

KING. It is my duty to my people.

FRED. Your people need you alive so that one day you can return.

KING. I will go alone. You take care of the English Lady.

FRED. Now, wait a minute. You can't go without saying goodbye to her. She has grown very fond of you. She'll be very upset.

KING. Well alright, but I cannot wait long.

FRED. You won't have to, just a few minutes. But you're missing a lot, you know, not going to England.

KING. Yes, I think I would like to go there one day.

FRED. I should think you would.

KING. Do you have sand in England?

FRED. Yes, but not as much as you do here.

KING. Do you have oil in your sand in England?

FRED. No, but we've got it on top of our sand in England! I'll tell you what we do have though, and I miss it more than anything else since I've been here. Green grass, fields, forests, parks . . . I'll tell you this, English kids have a whale of a time.

KING. Do they? Why?

FRED. Well, they go to the seaside. They eat ice-creams, candy-floss, toffee-apples, then they're sick.

KING. Do they go to the seaside on their camels?

FRED. Oh, we don't have camels.

KING. Do they say their prayers?

FRED. Of course.

KING. And does the English queen say her prayers.
(*The* KING *yawns*)

FRED. Of course.

KING. And all her husbands?

FRED. Our queen only has one husband.

KING. Oh, dear. When I grow up I can have as many wives as I want.

FRED. You may find one enough.
(The KING *is now nearly asleep)*

KING. Do you have a wife?

FRED. No, I don't.

KING. The English Lady is only pretending to be your wife?

FRED. Yes.

KING. Is that fun?

FRED. No.

KING. Oh, well, I think I would rather have a camel. *(falls asleep).*

FRED. I think you're a very good judge.
*(*HAMID *enters from Arch L.)*

HAMID. Mr. Florence!

FRED. Ssh!
(While he and FRED *speak,* FRED *intimates for* HAMID *to do the switch for the Reception Desk.* FRED *crosses beam and gently puts* KING *in Radio Room. He then revolves Radio Room off)*

HAMID. Quick, let us get away to the desert.

FRED. You rotten Arab!

HAMID. Are you not wanting to get away?

FRED. You'd leave everybody in the lurch? The King, the English lady, your wife?

HAMID *(after a pause).* Yes.
*(*HAMID *moves to go.* FRED *stops him)*

FRED. Come here.

HAMID. Captain Abu will soon discover all. Everyone will be shot.

FRED *(dramatically).* All right, Hamid. You save your own skin if you want to. Ride across the desert looking like a poor man's Tommy Cooper. I shall remain here and fight the forces of tyranny alone.

HAMID. And the best of British luck.
(*HAMID exits. FRED looks around and then takes out the lighter
and cigar that TRACY has given him earlier on. He thinks for a
moment where to put the cigar as an aerial and then sticks it in
his ear. He fiddles with the lighter and then speaks into it*)

FRED. See if this thing works. (*into lighter*). Can you hear me?
Fred to Lady Spence . . . I mean 'Come in Snow White . . . Can
you hear me, Snow White—this is DOPEY'.
(*He switches a knob on the lighter and puts it to his ear. He gets
no reply so he speaks into the lighter again. STAN has entered
and weaved his way downstairs. He is carrying his usual glass of
Brandy*)
(*into lighter*). Can you hear me? . . . Can you hear me? . . .
Can anybody hear me?

STAN (*who is now beside him*). Yes, I can hear you. Hello there.
(*FRED quickly puts the lighter in his pocket, STAN looks at the
cigar in FRED'S ear which FRED has forgotten. FRED smiles at
STAN*)
You feeling alright now?

FRED. Fine, fine.

STAN. Enjoyed that sing song.

FRED. Yes, indeed.
(*STAN has another glance at the cigar in FRED'S ear but isn't quite
sure whether to mention it or not*)

STAN. Yes. Bit of a surprise you going out of the window like that.

FRED. Yes, indeed.

STAN. Fell on your head, didn't you?

FRED. Yes, indeed.
(*STAN takes another look at the cigar and can restrain himself
no longer*)

STAN. I suppose it's silly to mention it.

FRED. What?

STAN. Well, I suppose you know it's there—

FRED. What?
(*STAN deliberates for a moment*)

STAN. You've got a cigar in your ear.
(*FRED remembers and nods*)

FRED. Yes.

STAN. Just thought I'd mention it.

FRED. Thank you.

STAN. Not at all, it's a pleasure.

FRED. I prefer to smoke them this way.

STAN. Oh.
(There is a pause while STAN empties his glass. He then takes out his lighter)
Would you like a light.
(FRED shakes his head)

FRED. No thanks. I'm trying to give them up.
(ELOISE enters from L.)

ELOISE. Feeling better, Sir John.

FRED. Much, thank you.

ELOISE. Still up and about, Mr. Charrington?

STAN. I'm not quite sure! Eloise, were you aware that Sir John smokes cigars through his ear-hole?

ELOISE. But of course.

STAN. I must be putting too much water with it. Are you sure you wouldn't like a light?

FRED. Yes, thanks.

STAN. Would you give me one then? I'm extremely obliged.
(He takes a cigar from his top pocket, puts it in his ear, and FRED lights it. STAN exits up stairs with smoke coming from cigar)

ELOISE. I'm so glad you decided to co-operate with us, M'sieur Florence.

FRED. I'm trying to, but I can't work this thing.

ELOISE. That is all right, Lady Spence is no longer transmitting. But I have already contacted her in the town, and the Major is getting a helicopter here as soon as possible.
(FARINA enters above. She is very angry and holding her bottom)
You take charge of the boy. Lady Spence will be here soon.

FARINA. Oh! So you are running away with that bird.
(FARINA comes down the stairs)

FRED *(to FARINA)*. What bird?

FARINA. The over-developed piece who jabbed my bum.

ELOISE. Go back to your room, girl!

FARINA. You keep out of this, you French faggot! I shall tell Captain Abu there's something fishy going on. And Mr. Wooley.

ELOISE. You must not do that!

FARINA. And who's going to stop me?

FRED. You go upstairs like a nice girl and I promise to explain it all later—
  (ELOISE unfastens brooch on her dress)

FARINA. I know you and your promises, Fred Florence.

FRED. Don't do it . . .!
  (But FARINA has already swung him round just as ELOISE jabs the brooch, which goes into FRED)

FARINA. Captain Abu, Captain Abu! (exits R.)

ELOISE (to FRED). Mon Dieu, what have I done to you?

FRED. You've jabbed my bum!

ELOISE. I must go after her. I will be back.
  (ELOISE swiftly exits D.L. FRED is reeling under the influence of the drug, as WAZIR comes down the stairs)

WAZIR. Ah, Sir John, thought I might have a nightcap. Will you join me, Sir John? As I always say to my father the General—
  (Suddenly FRED goes very stiff and grabs WAZIR'S jacket in a vice-like grip. FRED does not answer or move)

Let go of me, please—I insist. (beginning to get frightened). Let go—help!
  (WAZIR looks frantically around)

Help!
  (WAZIR first tries to release FRED'S hand from his jacket but to no avail)

You will please to let me go! Sir John?
  (WAZIR frees himself by removing his jacket, getting into the oddest positions. Finally, he manages it)

I will tell my father, the General.
  (TRACY enters hurriedly from L. as WAZIR exits R.)

TRACY. We must leave immediately. Where's Eloise—?
  (TRACY sees the odd expression on FRED'S face)

Mr. Florence this is no time to be playing games Mr. Florence—?
  (TRACY slaps his cheek, his jaw stays to the side but his expression still remains rigid)

FRED, what has happened?
  (TRACY slaps his cheek on the other side and his jaw shoots across and stays fixed.
  TRACY looks into his eyes)

You've been drugged. Swallow this.
 (*She removes a stone from her bracelet*)
It'll bring you round. Open your mouth.
 (**FRED** *sucks in his cheeks and makes a mouth like a goldfish.*
 TRACY *takes hold of his head and attempts to open his mouth*)
Say ah.

FRED. Mmm.

TRACY. Say ah.

FRED. Mmm
 (**TRACY** *slaps* **FRED's** *face. He opens his mouth.* **TRACY** *pops the pill in and* **FRED** *swallows it. He suddenly becomes a 'clockwork' soldier and marches off L. as* **FARINA** *and* **WOOLEY** *enter R.*)

TRACY. Fred, come back.

FARINA (*to* TRACY). Here, you've jabbed his bum as well, haven't you?

WOOLEY. I wish you'd refrain from using that expression, Miss Mahmoud.

FARINA. She did it to me as well, I tell you, she's dead kinky!

FRED (*enters, goes upstairs and walks into bedroom*). Ah, ah, ah ...

TRACY. Mr. Wooley, I'd better speak to you alone and I haven't much time.

FARINA. You watch her chum, or you'll get it up the ...

WOOLEY (*stopping her*). Yes, yes, yes. Lady Spence, from what I gather you were responsible for injecting a sharp object into this young lady's posterior.

FARINA. All this posh blinking talk. I'm getting the Colonel down here.

TRACY. No, you're not.

FARINA. Oh, yes I am, ducks.
 (**TRACY** *who has already taken out the syringe, jabs* **FARINA's** *backside*)
She's done it again! Look!

WOOLEY (*aghast*). You jabbed her bum.
 (**FARINA** *goes stiff and arms start to come up rigid*)
 (*to* TRACY). Lady Spence, have you gone out of your mind?
 (*As he says the word 'mind'* **FARINA** *grabs the tails of his jacket*)

TRACY. I suggest you leave immediately, Mr. Wooley.

WOOLEY (*still held by* FARINA). I shall do no such thing. I shall report your behaviour to the authorities.

TRACY. Mr. Wooley, I'm a member of British Intelligence.

WOOLEY. Nonsense!
(WOOLEY, *standing on tip-toe because of* FARINA *holding his jacket, picks up the telephone*)
(*on 'phone*). Operator! Operator!

TRACY. Don't do that, Mr. Wooley.
(TRACY *lifts her skirt*. WOOLEY *hurriedly turns his back on her*. TRACY *takes out an aerosol spray*)

WOOLEY (*on 'phone*). Operator! Ah! Give me the—
(TRACY *has sprayed* WOOLEY *with the aerosol*)
Give me—Give me— (*sings*). "Give me the Moonlight"—
(WOOLEY *starts to giggle*)
Goodbye, Operator.
(WOOLEY *is now convulsed with laughter and puts the 'phone back.*
The phone rings and WOOLEY *immediately picks it up*)
(*on 'phone*). Lyons Corner House here, Joe speaking. (*he laughs*)
. . . Hullo. Sir Bottomley-Joyless . . . Wooley? Yes, me's here . . .
Miss Entwhistle. Yes, she's here too. She's just had a thump up the bracket. (*he laughs*) . . . Drinking? Certainly not . . . I'm listening . . . Yes, all right, don't get your knickers in a twist.
(*He holds the 'phone away from his ear and giggles. He laughs and puts the 'phone down*)
(*over his shoulder to* FARINA). Stay with me, kid!
(WOOLEY *giggles*. TRACY *pulls* FARINA *out of the way*)

TRACY. Mr. Wooley, you realise I could have killed you just now?

WOOLEY. I know. (*to* FARINA). I do wish you'd cut your fingernails, Madame.

TRACY. I'd like you out of the way for the time being.

WOOLEY. What a splendid idea.
(*He opens clock door and gets in with* FARINA)
(*sings*). "Now is the Hour for me to say goodbye".

TRACY. Goodbye, Mr. Wooley.
(*She closes clock door on them*. ELOISE *enters from R.*)

ELOISE. Have you seen the troublesome FARINA?
(*The clock door opens and* WOOLEY *and* FARINA *are seen standing in the clock*)

WOOLEY. Cuckoo, cuckoo, cuckoo! (*he closes the door*).

TRACY. She's in the clock. Never mind about her. Let's get the king out of here and down to the village. The helicopter could arrive any time.

ELOISE. Is Monsieur Florence still drugged?

TRACY. He'll be alright, he's sleeping it off.

ABU (*off*). Get in there, you miserable fellow.

ELOISE. Captain Abu!

TRACY. Where's the King?

ELOISE. In the control room.

TRACY. Go to Mr. Florence. I've given him a pill but we may still need him.

(ELOISE *exits upstairs in bedroom, as* ABU *and* SOLDIER *enter with*

HAMID *between them.* WAZIR *is with them*)

ABU (*to* SOLDIER). Return to your post.
(*The* SOLDIER *exits Arch R.*)
(*to* HAMID). Now, why were you sneaking away into the desert?

HAMID. I was taking my camel for a walk.

ABU. At one o'clock in the morning.

HAMID. That is when my camel likes to go for a walk.

ABU. Would you say it was unusual for your camel to go out at one in the morning?

HAMID. All right. It is unusual for my camel to—

ABU. Get out!
(HAMID *jumps and exits L. The shutters of the bedroom open.*

FRED *and* ELOISE *look out*)

Lady Spence, I wish to see your son.

TRACY. I don't understand—

ABU. Immediately!

TRACY. But our son is asleep, Captain.

ABU. Then wake him up!

TRACY. To tell you the truth—

ABU. Yes?

TRACY. He has a slight cold.

ABU (*sharply*). Only one thing interests me at the present time. The King has escaped from the Capital.

TRACY. No!

ABU. To cross the border he will need to be disguised in some way—and he will need help. (*pointedly*). I will see your son now.

(FRED *and* ELOISE *close bedroom door*)

TRACY. It is ridiculous of course. (*to* WAZIR). You don't want to see our son, do you, Colonel?
(TRACY *has sidled up to* WAZIR)

WAZIR. No, I have no desire to see any of your family.

ABU. I insist on seeing the boy.

WAZIR. But why, Captain?

ABU. It is the General's order, Colonel.

WAZIR. Well, perhaps we had better see him. Orders is orders.

TRACY. But Roger has such a dreadful cold and a temperature. (*to* WAZIR). Do you really want to see him, darling?

WAZIR (*to* ABU). Do we, darling?—Captain.
(STAN *enters through curtained archway upstairs*)

ABU. Colonel, we must insist on seeing the boy.

STAN (*to* ABU). Something wrong, Captain?
(STAN *comes downstairs*)

ABU. That I cannot ascertain, Mr. Charrington. Suffice to say that I find the behaviour of everyone in this hotel odd in the extreme.

STAN. Nonsense. I've been staying here some time and I've never noticed anything odd.
(*The clock door opens and* WOOLEY *is seen with* FARINA)

WOOLEY (*singing*). "They're changing guard at Buckingham Palace. Christopher Robin went down . . ."
(*He laughs inanely.* ABU *is now almost beyond words*)

ABU. Mr. Wooley—what are you doing in there?
(WOOLEY *laughs louder*)

WOOLEY. I'm— (*he can't speak for laughter*). I'm—I'm passing the time away.
(*He hoots with laughter.* WOOLEY *closes the clock door*)

STAN. What a state to get into without resorting to liquor. Gracious me! I could have saved myself a fortune.

ABU. Lady Spence, I will see your son now.
(*The bedroom door opens and* ELOISE *hurries out and downstairs*)

ELOISE. Lady Spence, your poor Roger has the influenza I think. I will go for the doctor.

ABU (*stopping her*). No!

ELOISE. Captain, the little boy is—

ABU. No!

WAZIR. If the boy has a cold, Captain, perhaps—

ABU. Colonel—! (*choosing his words carefully*). If my theory is correct, there will be no cold because there is no English boy up here.
(*The bedroom shutters open and* FRED'S *head and shoulders appear at the window. He is wearing a woollen dressing gown and a schoolboy cap. He is holding a large handkerchief into which he sneezes violently. There is a pause while everybody takes in the situation.* FRED *sneezes again and* STAN *mops the top of his head*)

WAZIR. There you are, Captain.

ABU. Come down here, boy.
(FRED *sneezes again and the clock door opens*)

WOOLEY (*to* STAN). Bless you, sir.
(WOOLEY *closes clock door,* FRED *sneezes once again*)

TRACY. There you are, Captain—the boy has influenza.

STAN. Sounds more like a smoker's cough to me.

TRACY. He must go back to bed at once.

ABU. When we've had a look at him. Down here, boy!

FRED. Shan't.

ABU. I'll come up there then.

FRED. No. No. Coming down. (FRED *disappears as* WOOLEY *opens clock door*)

WOOLEY. At the 3rd stroke it will be one o'clock—LUNCHTIME!
(WOOLEY *closes door. The bedroom door opens and* FRED *rushes downstairs. As he reaches the bottom, he sneezes in* ABU's *face*)

ABU. Come here, boy.
(FRED *is now standing with his head on* TRACY'S *bosom, to the R. of* TRACY)

TRACY. It's all right, Roger.

WAZIR. Well, he's certainly not the King.

ABU. Alright, boy, I'm not going to hurt you.

TRACY. There, there.

WAZIR. How old did you say the boy was?

TRACY. Ten.

WAZIR. He's quite a big boy for ten, isn't he?
(FRED *makes himself smaller*)

STAN. You can see what he's after, can't you?

WAZIR. Does he want his mummy-wummy?
  (FRED *kicks* WAZIR'S *ankle*)
He's a real mother's boy, isn't he.

ABU. Show me your face.

FRED. Shan't. (FRED *moves to* L. *of* TRACY).

ABU. Show me your face. (FRED *kicks* ABU'S *ankle*).

TRACY. I'm so sorry, he's simply terrified of uniforms.

STAN. Been in trouble with the police, has he? You know, he reminds me of someone.
  (FRED *kicks* STAN'S *ankle. In fury* STAN *kicks* FRED *back and* FRED *drops the handkerchief which up till now he has used to cover his face*)

TRACY. Roger, you really must keep your hanky over your mouth!

STAN. Why not tie it round his bloody neck.

ABU. This has gone far enough. His father must be able to control him. Sir John! Sir John!

FRED (*dashing upstairs*). I'll get him. Daddy, Daddy!
  (*The clock door opens and* WOOLEY *can be seen together with* FARINA)

WOOLEY. You'll be happy to know that Miss Mahmoud and I have just become engaged.
  (*The bedroom door opens and* FRED *is standing there as Sir John Spence*)

FRED. What the deuce is going on?

ABU. I wish to see your boy.

FRED. That's impossible.

ABU. Why?

FRED. Don't change the subject.

ELOISE. You are being quite unreasonable, Captain.
  (FRED *bangs the door shut. The shutters open almost immediately and* FRED *appears as the little boy at the corner* L. *of the window*)

FRED (*high-pitched voice*). I feel sick!
  (FRED'S *head disappears and comes up the* R. *corner of window*)
(*as* Spence). The boy is terribly upset.
  (*He bobs down and comes up again on* L. *corner*)
(*high-pitched*). You're a great big bully!
  (*He bobs down and comes up again on* R. *corner as* ABU *walks*

into the bedroom. FRED *is unaware of this and continues with his business)*

(*as* Spence). The boy's had quite enough for one evening.

(ABU *can now be seen standing behind* FRED *as* FRED *bobs down and comes up at the L. corner of window)*

(*high-pitched*). I want to go wee-wee.

(*He bobs down and comes up again at the R. corner)*

(*as* Spence). How about that, Captain?—Captain?

(ABU *taps him on the shoulder and* FRED *turns to him)*

(*as* Spence). Ah, there you are. Can my little boy go— (*he suddenly realises*). Weee!

(ABU *makes a grab for* FRED *but* FRED *ducks and runs out along the landing. He exits through landing arch.* ABU *runs out of bedroom and stops at end of landing, not sure which way* FRED *has gone. As* ABU *looks out of the arched opening,* FRED *steps out of landing arch and shoves* ABU *out into the desert)*

WAZIR. Sir John!

(WAZIR *moves towards the stairs but* FRED *has already leapt out after* ABU. WAZIR *turns back to* TRACY)

Lady Spence, I demand to see your passport.

(TRACY *lifts her skirt, takes out the spray and squirts* WAZIR. WAZIR *repeats* WOOLEY'S *business and, as* HAMID *enters from Arch L. starts to fall forwards. In one deft movement and without stopping,* HAMID *catches him and carries him off L.)*

STAN (*with authority*). We're cutting it a bit fine, ladies. Take the King and wait for the helicopter at rendezvous 'X'.

(STAN *has operated the switch for the revolve and moves to cross the beam)*

TRACY. The King?

ELOISE. Helicopter?

TRACY. How do you know—?

STAN. My dear girl, I'm Bashful.

ELOISE. Bashful?

STAN. Second-in-Command Middle-East. You're doing a grand job.

(*He crosses the beam and the revolve comes round with the* KING *on it.* FRED *rushes in from Arch R.)*

FRED. We're for it now. Abu's got a squad of men coming up from the frontier post.

STAN. All speed, ladies. The back way.

TRACY. Your Majesty.

KING. When is something going to happen?

STAN. Eloise, the switch. Quick, the back way.
(The KING gets off the revolve and the Reception Desk returns as HAMID runs in from L.)

HAMID. At the back, two soldiers on guard.

FRED. We're surrounded.

STAN. Up on the roof. The helicopter will pick you up from there. I'll bluff it out with Abu.

FRED *(to TRACY, referring to STAN)*. What kind of pill did you give him?
(FRED, TRACY and the KING hurry upstairs and off)

STAN. Madame Agazi. Light up the flare on the roof for the helicopter.

ELOISE. Certainement.
(ELOISE hurries after the others and off)

STAN. Quickly, Hamid, you'd better go to the ladies.

HAMID. No thank you, I have already been.

STAN. I mean join the ladies!
(Exit HAMID upstairs)
(STAN leans against the reception desk and takes out his hip-flask as ABU marches in purposefully from arch R. followed by an Arab soldier.
ABU has a pistol and the soldier, a sten gun.
Around ABU'S forehead is a bandage and he is obviously suffering from a headache because of his fall. He also walks with a slight limp)

ABU *(to SOLDIER as he enters, in Arabic)*. Hurry, man. Follow me.

STAN *(very drunk again)*. Hullo, Captain!

ABU *(holding his head and wincing)*. Still drunk, Mr. Charrington?

STAN. So am I, isn't it lovely?
(ABU manages to contain himself)

ABU *(to SOLDIER)*. Search the rooms. Start up there.
(The SOLDIER goes upstairs and into the bedroom)
Mr. Charrington, where is Florence?

STAN. Italy.

ABU *(controlling himself)*. Where are Sir John and Lady Spence?

STAN. I really don't know.

ABU. Where is the son?

STAN. Should be coming over the horizon any minute now.
(ABU *is about to lose control as the* SOLDIER *comes out of the bedroom*)

SOLDIER. Nothing, Captain.

ABU (*in Arabic*). Search the other bedrooms.
(*The* SOLDIER *exits through arch landing*)

The hotel is surrounded, Mr. Charrington.
(ABU *gives a cursory glance through arch U.L.*
STAN *walks nonchalently upstairs during the next few lines*)

STAN. Good. Good. Good.

ABU. Neither Sir John nor Lady Spence will escape.

STAN. Splendid.

ABU (*moving to Arch D.L.*). Nor his Royal Highness.

STAN. Excellent.

ABU (*stops and turns*). Mr. Charrington, you think I know damn nothing! Well, let me tell you, I know damn all!

STAN (*grinning*). Yes, that's obvious.
(*The* SOLDIER *re-enters*)

SOLDIER (*in Arabic*). All the bedrooms are empty, Captain.

ABU (*to* STAN). Where are they?

STAN. Search me.
(ABU *raises his pistol*)

ABU. Mr. Charrington, I warn you. Already Sir John and Lady Spence are destined for the firing-squad.

STAN. Well, if the same fate befalls me, kindly see that my remains are donated to Ind, Coope and Allsop. And I hope they'll forgive me for having such a name as Charrington.
(*There is a sudden noise of a helicopter hovering overhead*)

ABU. What is that?

STAN. Flatulence!
(*The* SOLDIER *looks out of the window*)

SOLDIER. Captain, a helicopter.

ABU. Helicopter! (*in Arabic to* SOLDIER). Quick, outside!
(*The* SOLDIER *exits*)

(*To* STAN). Out of my way! (ABU *tries to get upstairs*)

STAN. Certainly.
(STAN *puts his foot into* ABU'S *chest and sends him flying.* STAN *rushes up the stairs but* ABU, *from the ground, fires his pistol.* STAN *catches his shoulder and wheels round*)

STAN. I say, steady on old man. That was a bit close.

ABU (*levelly*). Out of my way.

STAN. 'Fraid not, old fruit.

ABU. Please move. I give you five seconds.
(*A rope ladder from the helicopter drops into the courtyard behind* ABU)
One.
(FRED *appears climbing down the rope ladder*)

STAN. Ah, thank goodness. My dear friend Florence.
(ABU *doesn't turn round*)

ABU. An old trick, Mr. Charrington. Two.

STAN. Give him a gentle tap on the head as you go past, Fred.

ABU. It won't work. Three.

STAN. Hurry up, lad!
(FRED *is now behind* ABU)

ABU. Four.

STAN. Hit him, for God's sake!

FRED. What the hell with?!
(ABU *spins round and* FRED *snatches the pistol. He pretends to throw the gun to* STAN. ABU *turns round and* FRED *coshes him on the head with the pistol.* ABU *sinks to the ground*)

FRED (*calls up*). All systems go. Hurry up, Stan. Alright. Take it away.

(STAN *and* FRED *get on the bottom rung. The ladder starts to rise and the noise of the helicopter increases as*

THE CURTAIN FALLS.

The play was presented by Brian Rix Enterprises under the title of "Stand by your Bedouin" at the Garrick Theatre, London on March 15th 1967 with the following cast:—

SIR JOHN SPENCE	Kevin Frazer
AN ARAB BOY (THE KING)	Wendy Padbury
CAPTAIN SAREED EL DUR	Keith James
LADY TRACY SPENCE	Helen Jessop
HAMID	Andrew Sachs
ELOISE	Sheila Mercier
CAPTAIN ABU	Alan Tilvern
ARAB SOLDIER	John Newbury
HUBERT WOOLEY	Dennis Ramsden
FRED FLORENCE	Brian Rix
FARINA	Anna Dawson
STAN CHARRINGTON	Leo Franklyn
COLONEL WAZIR	Bill Treacher

Directed by WALLACE DOUGLAS.

N.B. If necessary the part of Sir John Spence may be doubled by the actor playing Colonel Wazir; and the Arab soldier may be doubled by the actor playing Captain Sareed El Dur.

DESCRIPTIONS OF CHARACTERS

SIR JOHN SPENCE	Tall, dark and handsome.
AN ARAB BOY (THE KING)	A pleasant little fellow.
LADY SPENCE	An attractive but very authoritative MI5 agent. Between 25-30.
HAMID	A frightened little man in his forties.
ELOISE	Hamid's French wife. A large strong-looking female. Aged about 40.
CAPTAIN ABU	A clever Arab Army Officer. He is *not* a bully but has quiet menace.
HUBERT WOOLEY	A bald headed pompous British official.
FRED FLORENCE	A not very good British Comedian. He is pleasant and perky. He can be North Country, Cockney, Scots or almost anything. Any age between 25-45.
FARINA	A voluptuous North Country girl about 25.
STAN CHARRINGTON	Aged about sixty. Permanently drunk but always likeable.
COLONEL WAZIR	A foolish Arab Officer who has been educated at Eton and Oxford.
ARAB SOLDIERS	An assortment.